BARRON'S DOG BIBLES

Labrador Retrievers

Joan Hustace Walker

SAGE Maslow

BARRON'S

Acknowledgments

This book would not be possible without the kind and generous help of members from the Labrador Retriever Club, and in particular, Sue Willumsen (Willcare Labradors) and Mary Wiest (Beechcroft Labradors) with the National Labrador Retriever Club. Also, a special thanks to Christine Neering, DVM, for lending her veterinary expertise and Labrador experience.

About the Author

Joan Hustace Walker is a member of the Dog Writer's Association of America (DWAA) and The Authors Guild. The author of 15 books and hundreds of articles, Walker has been nominated for 27 national awards, and has received the DWAA's coveted Maxwell Award six times, including the award for the 2006 Best Single Breed Book. Joan has been active in conformation, obedience, performance events, and rescue at various levels of participation for the past 30+ years. Joan has owned and trained Ginny, a rescue Lab, to whom she refers as her "heart" dog. She has been active in Greyhound rescue and currently owns two Rotts (one a rescue), and serves as chauffeur and pack mule for her daughter, Grace, as she travels the country showing her Havanese in the breed ring and in Juniors.

Dedication

To Ginny, my rescued Lab and "heart" dog.

All information and advice contained in this book has been reviewed by a veterinarian.

A Word About Pronouns

Many dog lovers feel that the pronoun "it" is not appropriate when referring to a pet that can be such a wonderful part of our lives. For this reason, Labrador Retrievers are described as "he" throughout this book unless the topic specifically relates to female dogs. This by no means infers any preference, nor should it be taken as an indication that either sex is particularly problematic.

Photo Credits

Kent Dannen: pages 2, 4, 8, 10, 17, 18, 21, 55, 59, 71, 74, 77, 80, 93, 104, 105, 109, 115, 116, 128, 132, 139, 142, 150, 155, 158, 160, 161, 162, 163, and 164; Tara Darling: page 178; Cheryl A Ertelt: pages 12, 141, and 174; Jean M. Fogle: pages 7, 57, and 60; Isabelle Francais: pages 19, 20, 23, 24, 29, 32 (top), 37, 38, 48, 54, 64, 66, 72, 75, 79, 85, 86, 89, 90, 97, 98, 100, 102, 107, 110, 111, 113, 119, 133, 135, 147, 153, 159, and 165; Karen Hudson: pages 3, 5, 13, 52, 62, and 94; Daniel Johnson: pages 120, 121, 122, 123, 124, and 125; Paulette Johnson: pages iv, 14, 30, 35, 41, 45, 47, 49, 50, 67, 83, 126, 130, 137, 146, 149, 156, and 166; Pets by Paulette: pages 6, 9, 25, 27, 33, 91, 95, 118, and 148; Shutterstock: pages i, iii, 32 (bottom), and 145

Cover Credits

Shutterstock: front and back cover.

All inquiries should be addressed to:
Barron's Educational Series, Inc.
250 Wireless Boulevard
Hauppauge, New York 11788
www.barronseduc.com

ISBN-10: 0-7641-6227-6 (Book)
ISBN-13: 978-0-7641-6227-5 (Book)
ISBN-10: 0-7641-8678-7 (DVD)
ISBN-13: 978-0-7641-8678-3 (DVD)
ISBN-10: 0-7641-9623-5 (Package)
ISBN-13: 978-0-7641-9623-2 (Package)

Library of Congress Catalog Card No: 2008042376

Library of Congress Cataloging-in-Publication Data
Walker, Joan Hustace, 1962–
    Labrador retriever / Joan Walker.
        p. cm.— (Barron's dog bibles)
    ISBN-13: 978-0-7641-6227-5
    ISBN-10: 0-7641-6227-6
    ISBN-13: 978-0-7641-8678-3
    ISBN-10: 0-7641-8678-7
    ISBN-13: 978-0-7641-9623-2
    ISBN-10: 0-7641-9623-5
    [etc.]
1. Labrador retriever. I. Title.

    SF429.L3W23 2009
    636.752'7--dc22

                                    2008042376

Printed in China

9 8 7 6 5 4

CONTENTS

CONTENTS

There is no question why the Labrador Retriever is the most popular breed in the world. Much of the breed's popularity has to do with his ability to excel in so many sports, activities, and service work, as well his capacity to adapt to so many different lifestyles. The Labrador is a willing, eager learner with a great nose, an intense focus, and a big, friendly temperament that makes him not only fun to train but also a joyful companion.

Living with a Lab, of course, is not without its challenges. When people purchase a sweet, soft yellow, black, or chocolate puppy, they often don't consider how more than 100 years of selectively breeding for the ultimate hunting dog will affect their companions' behaviors in the home. Even if the puppy doesn't come from recent hunting lines, he still possesses generations of breeding for birdiness, retrieving, endurance, courage, and an inherent desire to *work* with someone. These characteristics are ingrained in his genetic makeup, and he will display "gundog" behaviors, whether you want him to be a hunting dog or not.

If, as a prospective Lab owner, you understand how years of breeding for hunting have shaped the Lab's inherent characteristics, you can much better determine if the Labrador Retriever is the dog for you. And armed with that knowledge, you will go into Lab ownership with a plan for how you are going to meet your new Labby's needs (lots of exercise, solid training, and regular attention).

If the Lab's basic needs are met, and you enjoy working with him, he will make an excellent companion. If the dog's needs aren't met or if the amount of walking, training, and time with the dog is an enormous sacrifice, there will be a disconnect. The Lab will find himself banished to the backyard or relinquished to a shelter for simply doing what pent-up, untrained, neglected Labs do best (leave a wake of destruction in their paths).

What determines whether a Labrador Retriever succeeds or fails in a home depends not on the dog. . . but on the owner. You are the determining factor as to whether your Labby makes it or breaks it in your home. Unless you've owned Labs before, knowing how a Labrador is going to behave in the home is literally a complete unknown.

Until now . . . this Labrador Retriever book is different because its purpose is to bare all. You want to know the good, the bad, and the ugly of this breed? It's all here. And if, after understanding how the Labby is going to affect your life, your household, your family, and your friends, you *still* want to own a Lab, then read on!

Within this book are tons of great tips and tricks for taking care of everything from that first night home with a new puppy or dog, to health care, grooming, and training. There's even a chapter devoted to caring for the specific needs of the senior Labrador. A comprehensive resource chapter at the end provides additional contact information for organizations, as well as scores of books that can provide more in-depth information on many different topics. It is hoped that this volume will be the resource you'll use throughout your Lab's life.

Chapter One

All About the Labrador Retriever

The Labrador Retriever has reigned supreme as the most popular dog in the world for more than a decade. With annual registrations topping 114,000 dogs in 2007, Labrador Retrievers have maintained the position as the number one breed in the United States for more than 17 consecutive years. Of course, the Lab wasn't always "top dog." His rise in popularity took nearly a century to take flight.

Origins of the Labrador Retriever

The Labrador Retriever is considered an English breed, which is a bit confusing, because "Labrador" is immediately north of Newfoundland and is now a province of Canada.

Want to muddy the waters a bit more? Early ancestors of the Labrador Retriever weren't even from Labrador; they were from Newfoundland.

Confused yet? Hang on, there's more. Newfoundland didn't have any indigenous dogs; any dogs that were developed in Newfoundland (including the Newfoundland) were a result of importing dogs from . . . England and Europe.

So, the early, not-so-simple history of the Labrador Retriever is that he is named for a place that he didn't originate in, and that his earliest ancestors came from England and Europe, went to Newfoundland (where he was refined into an excellent retrieving dog), then came back to England, where he was further developed and refined until he finally became the Labrador Retriever that we mostly recognize today.

That was simple, wasn't it? The longer history goes a little bit like this.

Back and Forth Across the Atlantic

The earliest dogs used to develop the all-purpose retriever/fisherman's dog in Newfoundland are thought to have come to the island when it was first settled in the late 1500s by the British. Over the next 200 years, additional dogs would come into Newfoundland from British and European fishing boats.

Though it would seem today to be a *long* way to sail for some fish, Newfoundland was the shortest distance between England and Europe

and North America (1,600 miles from Ireland). Additionally, the cold waters surrounding Newfoundland were teeming with fish, making it worthwhile for fishermen to come from as far away as France, Spain, and Portugal.

Along with those fishermen came a variety of retrievers and water spaniels, which were handy to have on board not only for their working skills but also as companionship. The English and European retrievers and spaniels that found their way to Newfoundland were likely of a variety of colors, body shapes, and sizes, as well as possessing a variety of coat types: short coated, flat coated, long haired, and curly coated.

Of course, centuries ago there weren't refrigerator units or ice chests in the holds of ships. Any fish that were caught by foreign boats needed to be dried (and salted) before making the return journey home. Foreign fishing boats would stay for a season of fishing, hauling in their catch and curing fish on the shores of Newfoundland, giving locals plenty of time to purchase, barter for, or breed their dogs to foreign dogs.

Fun Facts

The name Labrador Retriever is thought to have originated in the early 1800s when a British nobleman mistakenly referred to the dogs as being from Labrador, as opposed to Newfoundland.

A Cold-water Retriever Takes Shape

Before the 1800s, dogs weren't bred to have a certain look, color, or body style *unless* that look, color, or body style served a function or made the dog better at his job. So, the breeding efforts of the Newfoundlanders actually

FYI: Newfoundland vs. St. John's

The differences between the "Newfoundland" and the "St. John's" dog were described in *Instructions to Young Sportsmen*, written in 1814 by sportsman Colonel Peter Hawker (1786–1853): "The one is very large; strong in the limbs; rough haired; small in the head; and carries his tail very high. He is kept in the country for drawing sledges full of wood, from inland to the sea shore, where he is also very useful, by his immense strength and sagacity, among wrecks, and other disasters in boisterous weather."

"The other, and by far the best for every kind of shooting, is oftener black than of another colour, and scarcely bigger than a pointer. He is made rather long in the head and nose; pretty deep in the chest; very fine in the legs; has short or smooth hair; does not carry his tail so much curled as the other; and is extremely quick and active in running, swimming, or fighting."

Additional excerpts from the book and from Hawker's diary can be accessed at: *www.poodlehistory.org/HAWKER.htm*

produced two distinct types of dogs: the Newfoundland, a larger dog that assisted with fishing tasks and pulled carts; and a smaller dog that also assisted with fishing tasks but could serve as a good gundog, too. The "form" or body style of these two ensuing breeds, therefore, *came* from developing the dog's function.

With icy cold waters the norm in Newfoundland year-round, the form that began to take shape for the island's smaller, working retriever included qualities that made the dog a good swimmer (broad chest, buoyant body, and webbed feet), and a resilience to cold water (an efficient distribution of body fat, as well as a thick, water-resistant double coat).

Another physical feature of the dog that began to appear was that of an "otter" tail. Rather than having a tail that was held curled over the back, the retriever from Newfoundland had a rudder-like tail: thick, shorter (more of a three-quarter-length tail), mostly straight and held lower. Early records note that the retriever was primarily black in color, and was sometimes referred to by many names, including St. John's Water Dogs and Little Newfoundlers.

As word spread of the abilities of the black retriever from Newfoundland, sportsmen in England sat up and took notice. The exact date that St. John's Water Dogs were first imported into England isn't known; however, early

records indicate that sometime between 1825 and 1830, dogs were received by the Fifth Duke of Buccleuch, his brother Lord John Scott, the Earl of Malmesbury, the Earl of Home, and a "Mr. Radclyffe."

The imported St. John's dogs were so highly valued that by 1880, it is estimated that more than 60 gamekeepers were training and looking after Labrador Retrievers on different estates in England.

Breed Truths

The Labrador was not the first retriever to be recognized by the AKC. The Chesapeake Bay Retriever holds that honor, with recognition in 1878.

However, the supply of St. John's dogs was soon to be all but cut off. Newfoundland inaugurated a Sheep Protection Act, which imposed a duty on all dogs, so fewer people could afford to keep and breed dogs. Added to this problem, England initiated its Quarantine Act. So, by 1885, not only had the number of St. John's dogs dwindled severely in Newfoundland, but it was far more difficult (if not impossible) to import dogs into England.

The breeding and future of the Labrador Retriever now lay in the hands of England. Thankfully, dedicated British sportsmen and dog fanciers continued to breed and refine the Labrador. In 1903, the breed was recognized by the Kennel Club of the United Kingdom.

Retriever Recognition

Interestingly, in the early days of dog showing, retrievers used to be exhibited in Kennel Club shows *together*. In other words, there were no separate classes for Golden Retrievers, Flat-Coated Retrievers, Curly-Coated Retrievers, or Labs. Rather, dogs were shown in a retriever class by their coat type (i.e., flat, curly, etc.). It wasn't until 1905 that the Labrador was recognized as a separate breed and classified as a "sub-variety" of retriever.

Of course, this classification still had its issues, as dog owners were allowed to register their dogs under the breed that it most closely resembled—whether or not the dog was pure Labrador Retriever, mostly Lab, or another retriever breed entirely. To sort this out, the Labrador Retriever Club was founded in England in 1916 and a breed standard was drawn up that outlined precisely how the Labrador was to look and move, and what its characteristics and

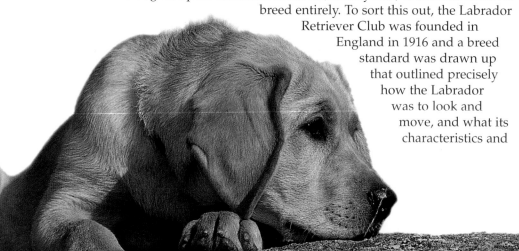

temperament traits were to be. This breed standard has undergone few changes in the past 90-plus years, mainly to further clarify and more fully describe the original description.

Aristocratic Entry into the States

Word of the talented Labrador Retriever quickly spread to sportsmen in America and Canada. Two years after the Labrador Retriever was recognized as a sub-variety of retriever in England, the Lab was recognized by the Canadian Kennel Club (CKC). Twelve years later in 1917, the Labrador was recognized by the American Kennel Club (AKC).

It's hard to imagine that the breed that is enjoyed and treasured today by more people than any other was once owned and bred by so few in the United States. The gentlemen's sport of shooting, made popular in Scotland, became a passion among America's elite in the 1920s. Wealthy individuals would not only import Labrador Retrievers from English kennels, but would also bring over young Scottish gamekeepers to help develop and run shooting preserves on their sprawling estates.

Though the number of Labrador Retrievers in the United States was very low initially, the Labrador Retriever Club, Inc. was formed in 1931. It was in that same year that the first AKC-sanctioned field trial was held.

Fun Facts

Labrador Firsts

Mr. Lord's Boli of Blake—first Labrador Retriever to earn an American conformation championship (1933); Blind of Arden—first American Labrador Retriever Field Champion (1936).

FYI: National Labrador Retriever Club

In addition to the Labrador Retriever Club, there is another national breed club. The National Labrador Retriever Club was organized in 1996 and promotes the international Labrador Retriever breed standard, which is set by the Fédération Cynologique Internationale (FCI). The FCI breed standard is the standard that is accepted and used by 80 countries throughout the world when judging the Labrador Retriever.

The superb hunting abilities of the Labrador attracted a wide following, and it wasn't long after those first field trials were held in the United States that American sportsmen gained a keen interest in the breed. From the late 1930s to the late 1970s, the Lab enjoyed a gradual, controlled climb in popularity and was a favored breed among competitive field trialers as well as those seeking an excellent personal hunting dog. The Labrador Retriever was also quite successful in the show ring (conformation).

In the early 1980s, pet owners realized just how friendly, sociable, and easily trained the Lab was. It is at this point that the Lab's popularity skyrocketed and the breed made the jump from favored retriever to favored household pet. Fortunately, the good-natured Lab proved to be highly adaptive and, for the most part, has performed his most recent starring role as a pet very well.

Rise in Fame as a Working Dog

Pet owners weren't the only folks who realized the Labrador Retriever's potential outside of marshes and fields. Service dog organizations that traditionally used German Shepherds for trained assistance dogs for the blind or disabled began to shift their breeding programs to include Labrador Retrievers. Today, roughly 60 to 70 percent of service dogs are Labrador Retrievers. The dogs are revered for their willingness to work, friendliness toward people, and high level of comfort in crowds and when presented with loud noises.

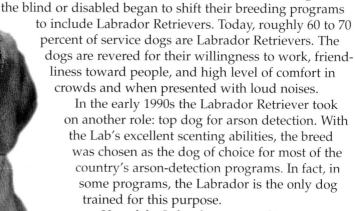

In the early 1990s the Labrador Retriever took on another role: top dog for arson detection. With the Lab's excellent scenting abilities, the breed was chosen as the dog of choice for most of the country's arson-detection programs. In fact, in some programs, the Labrador is the only dog trained for this purpose.

Use of the Labrador as a working, scent-detection dog grew. In 1999, the Transportation Security Administration

(TSA) founded a kennel to breed its own Labrador Retrievers for explosives-detection work. The program began with six adult female Labs and two adult males, selected specifically for their scenting abilities, trainability, work ethic, temperament, and health. Today the program produces nearly 300 trained Labradors annually for placement in the TSA program.

As other K9 programs expanded to include single-purpose dogs (the dogs were not required to perform patrol dog duties, such as apprehending criminals, and could focus strictly on scenting), more and more Labradors entered scent-detection programs for police, military, and government agencies.

Working Labrador Retrievers are used to scent out everything from smuggled money, narcotics, illegally imported plants, and explosives to finding trapped or missing people, and serving in recovery missions. Many of the search-and-rescue dogs employed in the aftermath of the 2001 terrorist attacks on the Pentagon and the Twin Towers in New York were Labrador

Breed Truths

What are Gundogs?

Gundogs fall into three classifications: retrievers, pointing dogs, and flushing spaniels. Retrievers retrieve birds that have been shot. Pointers and setters find birds and indicate the location of a bird in the grass or underbrush by literally making a big arrow with their bodies. Spaniels flush birds out of the field by zigzagging or "quartering" through the brush and undergrowth to drive birds up into the air for a hunter to shoot.

Retrievers, working for volunteer SAR organizations, as well as police, fire-fighters, the military, and other government agencies.

Understanding the Lab's Purpose

Upland game . . . waterfowl . . . blind and marked retrieves . . . gundogs . . . retrievers . . .. If you're not familiar with the hunting world, these words may be a bit foreign—and, as a result, the "job" that has evolved for the Labrador Retriever may be a bit of a mystery to the nonhunting pet owner.

FYI: Labs Around the World

Country	First Year Recognized; Registry	National Breed Club	Registration Numbers 2007	Current Popularity	Years in #1 Position
United States	1917; American Kennel Club	Labrador Retriever Club, Inc.	114,113	#1	17
England	1903; Kennel Club of the United Kingdom	Labrador Retriever Club	45,079	#1	16
Canada	1905; Canadian Kennel Club	Labrador Retriever Club of Canada	8,881	#1	8

A Lab is first and foremost a retriever. He fetches. While waiting by the hunter's side, the good Lab watches the fall of a shot bird, "marking" its placement in his mind so that he knows precisely where to go when he is asked to retrieve it.

But of course, nothing is quite as simple as just running out and bringing a dead duck back to a hunter. Sometimes the Lab sees where the bird falls (a "marked" retrieve) and other times he doesn't (a blind retrieve). Or, the dog may see one bird's fall but not a second or third bird shot at nearly the same time.

In a "blind" retrieve, the hunter helps send the dog into the general area of where the bird fell (i.e., go left, a little more right, farther, come back a little, etc.). Hunters teach their dogs to turn or move according to short and long whistle blasts, voice commands, and hand signals. When the dog gets close to the fallen bird, he uses his scenting abilities to close the deal.

With bird in mouth, the Labrador is now to return to his handler as quickly as possible without damaging the goods. The first-rate retriever has a very "soft" mouth; dogs that grip the bird too tightly are considered to have "hard" mouths and can damage the meat. Once back to the hunter, the Lab gives the bird "to hand" or directly to the hand of the hunter. If multiple birds have been shot, the Lab is sent out to go and retrieve each bird individually.

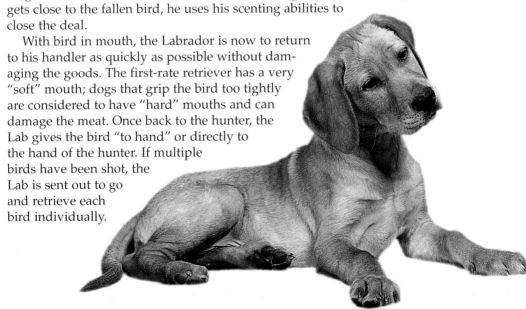

The Labrador Retriever is considered an excellent personal hunting companion; he embodies the best of all retriever characteristics and is equally strong retrieving on land as in water. To do his job well, the Lab was bred to have infinite patience (it might take a while to find a bird to shoot), terrific scenting abilities (allowing the dog to better find the location of a fallen bird or track a wounded bird), tremendous courage (necessary to forge through thick underbrush and jump unflinchingly into cold water), boundless energy (the dog needed to be able to hunt all day), and a strong, innate retrieving drive.

Labrador Retrievers in Art and Entertainment

When tracking a purebred dog's evolution, breed historians often turn to early works of art.

The first known Labrador Retriever work of art, *Cora: A Labrador Bitch*, by noted British artist Sir Edwin Landseer (1802–1873) was exhibited at the British Institution in 1822, under the title *Watchful Sentinel*. The dog featured in the painting has a heavy black coat, feathering on a longish tail, and white markings on her legs and chest. *Cora* is an attractive dog, but her conformation is far removed from what we would consider a Labrador Retriever today. In fact, if the painting's title hadn't included *Labrador*, a viewer wouldn't have suspected that the subject of the painting was an early ancestor of today's Labs.

Landseer's work is important, however, in that it shows just how varied the Labrador was in color, coat, and body type when it was initially imported into England. It also sets a marker for how far the breed progressed in a matter of a few generations—which can be noted in later paintings by other noted artists.

For example, roughly fifty years later, the Labrador looks very much like it does today in a painting titled *Frank: A Black Labrador Retriever,* by British artist George Earl (1824–1908).

Another work, *Labrador Retrieving Rabbit,* by Earl's daughter, Maud Earl (1864–1942), shows the utility of this breed, proving that not only could he retrieve upland birds and waterfowl, but that the Lab was used frequently to retrieve small game, too.

Other notable artists who captured the beauty and spirit of the Labrador include the following:

- **American artist Arthur F. Tait (1819–1905):** Known for his sporting art, Tait portrays a beautiful black Lab in the painting *Gray Horse and Bay in Stable Interior with Black Labrador.*
- **Arthur Wardle (1864–1949):** A British artist who was recognized for his paintings of terriers, Wardle featured a black Lab with three spaniels and two pheasants in the work *Looking Ahead.*
- **George Vernon Stokes (1873–1954):** Stokes was another British artist, and his 1938 drawing of a Labrador Retriever is featured in the book *Sporting Dogs, London & NY,* by A. Croxton-Smith.
- **Reuben Ward Binks (1880–1980):** A British artist famous for his sporting paintings, Binks completed many portraits of famous Labradors, such as *Ch Titus of Whitmore and Ch Tag of Whitmore* (1927), a British dual champion (field and conformation) and a British field champion respectively; and *Bramshaw Bob Swimming,* a painting of British Dual Champion Bramshaw Bob retrieving a bird. (Bramshaw Bob was also a Best in Show winner at Crufts in 1932 and 1933.)

Fun Facts

Presidential Pups

Buddy, a chocolate Labrador puppy, came to the White House to live with President Bill Clinton; and Jackson and Dave (black and yellow Labradors respectively) graced the grounds of the U.S. Naval Observatory while Dick Cheney served as vice president. In Russia, former Russian President Vladimir Putin's black Lab, Koni, was so popular with the press corps that Putin had to ask journalists and photographers to please refrain from feeding the friendly canine biscuits and other treats.

Labrador Retrievers have also made it onto the large screen appearing in numerous television shows, commercials, and movies. A few "famous" Labs you might remember include the Advantix puppy (a yellow Lab puppy who sings sweetly that you won't find any fleas on him), and Vincent from the television series *Lost.* (Vincent is actually a female Lab, Madison, who wears hair extensions.)

Labradors are a bit scarce as main characters in movies, but the following are some movies where a Lab played a significant role: *The Incredible Journey* (1963), *Rascal* (1969), *Far From Home: The Adventures of a Yellow Dog* (1994), *The Santa Clause* (1994), *The River Wild* (1994), *Independence Day* (1996), *Volcano* (1997), and more recently *Marley & Me* (2008).

Labrador Retriever Colors

Labs come in three colors: black, yellow, and chocolate. Historically, black has been the predominant color among Labrador Retrievers, and in the earliest days of the breed, it was also the most desirable color. White markings do appear on black Labs, particularly on the chest, toes, pads of the paws, and chin. Anything larger than a small spot on the chest, however, is a disqualification in the show ring.

Yellow Labs have been around for more than a century: The first registered yellow Labrador, Ben of Hyde, was born to an otherwise all-black litter in 1899 from the noted British kennels of Major C. J. Radclyffe. Yellow Labs range in color from a creamy, nearly white color to a very rich yellow with red-fox coloring. The yellow Lab's lips, nose, and eye rims are black; however, a yellow Lab's nose can get a pinkish cast to it. Dogs that are born with black noses can lighten up with age and in colder climates; in rare cases, a yellow Lab is born with a pink nose *and* has pink or chocolate coloring around the eyes (as opposed to black eye rims). A yellow Lab without black pigment is called a Dudley, and cannot be shown in the breed ring.

Chocolate, a color that was reportedly present in St. John's dogs, was first recorded in Labrador Retrievers in 1892 with a litter that was born to the

Scottish kennels of the Sixth Duke of Buccleuch; however, it wasn't until the 1930s that the color began to gain favor. Chocolate Labs can range from a café au lait coloring to a deep liver color. Chocolate Labradors have brown eye rims, lips, and noses. Of the three colors, chocolate continues to be the least recorded of colors in the Labrador Retriever.

Mismatched Colors

Occasionally, some rather wild color combinations occur in the Labrador Retriever. Remember, many breeds went into the development of the breed and every so often, if both parents have a recessive gene for a certain type of coloring lurking in their genetics, a surprising array of colors and markings might show up.

Referred to as "mismarks," some of the unusual colors and combinations that can be seen in purebred Labrador Retrievers include brindles (also known as "splash"), tan markings (black or chocolate dogs with tan points), yellows with black spots, yellow and black dogs with a white ring around the tail, and even some dogs with larger mismatched colors, such as a yellow dog with a big splotch of black on the shoulder or a black dog with one yellow leg. It almost looks like someone splashed a bit of paint on the dog.

Though these variations in coat color are very interesting and very rare, they are *not* desirable and are disqualifying traits in the show ring. In other words, these puppies are not worth *more* for their coloring. To see photos of these mismatched colors visit *www.woodhavenlabs.com/mismarks.html*

Labs Today

The Labrador Retriever earned the number one position in the world because he is, without question, a great dog. Today's Lab is not only tops as a family pet but continues to reign supreme as a retriever and personal gundog. The Lab is also a top choice in police, fire, government, and military work as a detection dog, and in the private sector as a tremendous assistance and service dog.

The characteristics that have made the Labrador such a popular breed for the past several decades have not changed among well-bred dogs: The classic Lab is intelligent and eager to learn, a tireless worker and a solid retriever, and possesses a bomb-proof temperament. He is a dog that can adapt to a variety of living situations and is adept at participating in a huge range of performance events and outdoor activities.

Chapter Two

The Mind of the Labrador Retriever

The Labrador is a versatile, congenial dog of medium to large size that's not huge, and definitely not too small. He is quite adaptable to a variety of living situations, and as long as his needs are met, the Lab can be a good fit in many homes.

The World According to the Labrador Retriever

Though the Labrador Retriever is most frequently seen as a pet, today's Lab still possesses the genetics for all the abilities of his forefathers. Within the breed there is great variance as to the intensity of each individual Labrador Retriever's abilities and drives; however, even Labs that haven't been bred for field work in generations will still possess certain characteristics in common with their superior hunting relatives.

What does this mean? You can take the Lab out of hunting, but you can't really take "hunting" out of the Lab. It's in there to some extent. More than 100 years of breeding have been focused on developing the ideal hunting dog, so just because people now desire the dog as a pet, doesn't mean all these inherent abilities, intense drives, and temperament traits simply go away.

This in no way means that the Labrador isn't a great dog. In fact, if an owner knows what the inherent traits of a Lab are and how they could potentially affect home life when the Lab is strictly a pet (and not actively competing in the field or hunting on weekends), the owner will be better equipped to predict the impact of the new dog on his or her life. Knowing what to expect makes it easier for dog owners to determine if the Labrador Retriever is truly the dog for them.

Pros and Cons

Every breed has its benefits and challenges, and the Lab is no different in this aspect. There are qualities of the Labrador Retriever that make him an incredible dog to own, and there are parts of this dog that can make him difficult to live with in certain circumstances.

Whether the Lab is a good fit for *you* depends a lot on how highly you value the strong points of the breed versus how you handle the more challenging aspects of the breed. How you view the strengths and weaknesses of this breed depends on your lifestyle, your living situation, your expectations for a dog, and countless other factors. Only you can decide if the Labrador is a good choice for you.

To help you make up your mind, here's a list of some of the good points of the breed and some of the facets of the Labrador that some dog owners have found a bit more challenging.

Breed Truths

Though the Labrador Retriever is eager to spend the day outside with you, don't think this means he'll be equally eager to spend the day outside *without* you. Labs love their people and are happiest when they can be with their families as *house dogs*, never as "backyard" dogs.

What's Good About the Labrador

There's an awful lot of "good" going on with this breed. These are just a few of the Labrador Retriever's finer points.

Good-natured The Lab is renowned for his congenial temperament. Easygoing and friendly, the Labrador is generally very stable in his temperament and often well suited for the novice owner to raise.

Easy to Train No dog trains himself; however, the Labrador Retriever is exceptionally bright *and* eager to please his owner, making him an ideal dog to work with on house manners and obedience skills.

Athletic If you're looking for a dog to go jogging with, a hiking companion, or a breed that can partake in a variety of sports (both competitive and recreational), the healthy Labrador Retriever won't disappoint.

Family Dog Some breeds are very much a one-person dog—they bond closely with one individual and may or may not be tolerant of other family members. The Lab tends to love his entire family.

Low-maintenance Coat The Labrador Retriever's coat does not require expensive clips or professional grooming to maintain. If you can use a brush and don't mind bathing him occasionally, you can keep a Lab's coat in good shape.

Swimmer Extraordinaire Water activities are right up this dog's alley. If introduced to water in a gentle manner, this breed is a great choice for a person who likes to spend time at the beach or lake.

Dog-friendly Successful hunting dogs must be able to get along with other dogs working in the field. This translates to a breed that typically isn't dog aggressive.

All-around Hunting Dog The Labrador Retriever will retrieve on land and in water. A dog from hunting or "field" lines can make a terrific personal hunting companion.

Loves People With proper socialization, the Labrador Retriever is very accepting of strangers and is more likely to show an intruder the way to the cookie jar than pin him in a corner.

Good with Kids The well-bred Labrador is quite tolerant (he's not as easily offended as other breeds might be with an accidental bump or tug) and can be a great companion for responsible children.

What's Challenging About the Labrador

Many of the Labrador Retriever's traits as a hunting dog can translate into higher demands as a house pet. None of these characteristics is insurmountable; however, they may require you to make a few adjustments in the home or to your lifestyle.

High Exercise Requirements The Labrador Retriever was bred to *go* all day in the field, hunting. The exercise demands of the Labrador from puppy through young adulthood and beyond (at least the first four years) are usually what shock new Lab owners the most. In general this dog will require a half hour to an hour of serious exercise *at least* twice a day.

Demands Attention The Lab was bred to work with, not independent of, a hunter. In a home, this translates to a dog that requires interaction with his owner. He will shadow you. He will bring you toys. He will even resort to inappropriate behaviors, if that's what it takes to get your attention.

Exercising (with you), training (with you), and attention (from you) will all help to keep your Labby happy.

Mental Challenges A smart dog is great for training, but an intelligent dog can become destructive if you don't stimulate him mentally. Labs need to see new things, go to different places, and smell fresh scents. They need to learn new skills. If your Lab gets bored, he will try to find ways to entertain himself, and nine times out of ten, you won't be entertained with what he comes up with . . . .

Destructiveness If the Lab's physical (exercise), mental (training), and emotional (attention) needs are not met, he tends to be quite destructive. Chewing everything, shredding pillows and furniture, digging trenches in the backyard, jumping the fence, and barking are just a few of the ways he'll express himself.

CAUTION

If a Lab can get his mouth around an object, it is very likely that he can swallow it. The most commonly "surgically retrieved" items include tennis balls and socks.

Slime The Labrador is a great retriever. Some dogs have "wetter" or more slobbery mouths than others. If you've got a slobberer, you'll find a nice, thick coat of slime on everything he chews or carries.

Costly Health Problems Many of the aging Labrador Retriever's ailments can be chronic and expensive to treat. Arthritis medications can cost upward of 4 to 5 dollars a day; foods designed for dogs with allergies can cost 80 dollars or more a month; and lipomas, or fatty tumors, though generally not dangerous, can be quite unattractive, and if surgical removal is required, can cost hundreds of dollars per surgery.

Hair, Hair Everywhere The Labrador Retriever's thick, double coat is terrific protection from the elements while hunting and good insulation for dives into lakes. The downside is that this coat sheds constantly. If you think you know how much hair this is, visit a Lab owner's home *before* they've vacuumed. A single dog can shed more hair in one day than most people can imagine.

Physical Players The Lab has a very physical manner of play: Chasing, wrestling, and body slamming are typical maneuvers among friendly, boisterous dogs. If you've got small children or older kids who tend to run and play hard themselves, you'll need to take precautions to make sure that both dog and children know the rules and boundaries at playtime.

Require Training Because of the Labrador's size and, shall we say, gusto for life, he is an exuberant companion. The Lab requires a good grounding in house rules and basic obedience commands just to keep him controllable when he's happy and/or excited. Don't forget, too, that the courage needed to dive unflinchingly into brambles, deep cover, and ice cold water can also translate into a dog that can be a bit pushy at times. Daily training, even just ten minutes a day with all family members, is usually all that is needed to maintain a healthy leadership relationship with the pet Lab.

Breed Truths

The drive to retrieve can be so great in some Labs that they won't stop even when they are exhausted. Owners need to monitor these dogs' activity—particularly in hot weather—to keep them safe.

Odor All dogs produce some oil in their coats; however, breeds such as the Lab that were developed for water activities generally produce *more* oil. This creates a distinct smell, which is particularly obvious when the dog has been exerting himself outside or becomes wet. If you find the smell particularly offensive, you will need to be prepared to wash your Lab more frequently (but not so frequently that it dries out the dog's skin).

Poor Temperaments Whenever a dog hits the number one position in popularity, it is a given that the breed's naturally agreeable temperament will be corrupted by people who are more interested in how many puppies they can sell than how *good* a puppy they can produce. For this reason, a puppy buyer cannot *assume* that a puppy will have a tremendous temperament just because he is a Lab.

BE PREPARED! Are You Committed?

Statistically, most dogs that wind up at shelters come from multi-pet households. Multi-pet households can be more challenging to manage, so before adding a dog to your home make sure you have the time, patience, and commitment to make the situation work.

Needs a Job A dog that was bred for generations to perform a specific working function (in the case of the Labrador, hunting), requires regular mental and physical activity. This does not mean that you have to hunt your Labrador, but you will need to keep him busy.

Labradors as Family Dogs

The Labrador Retriever is the country's most popular breed in large part because he makes such a good family dog. We place higher expectations on our dogs today than we did decades ago. The job description of "family dog" has become more demanding than that of many true, working canine jobs.

The family dog is expected to be nonreactive to pokes, prods, and pinches from small children. He is expected to know when to welcome friends into the home and when to warn that a suspicious stranger is approaching. He is expected not to snap when someone falls on him or be protective of his toys, food, or crate. The family dog is to know his place in the family and never test the waters or try to move up in that ranking. Oh yes, and the family dog is expected to be accident-free in the house, play well with all dogs, and come when called.

There are dogs that fit this ideal. And, it's pretty safe to assume that many of these dogs are Labrador Retrievers; however, a Lab doesn't become the perfect family dog without help from his owner.

With that said, can the Labrador make a good family dog? Absolutely! The most common concern with Lab puppies and kids is the robustness of the puppy's play. Of course, if the pup gets enough exercise and knows his basic commands, even this usually poses no problems. Labrador Retrievers have a natural affinity toward children, but that doesn't make them automatically *good* with children—or vice versa, for that matter. Both dog and child need to be taught how to behave with each other, what is allowable and what is not.

Basically it's this: If the Lab puppy is raised with respectful children and is given rules that are fair and consistently enforced, he will mature into a wonderful family member.

Adult Labs, those that are adopted from a rescue, can be excellent with children, too. In fact, an adult Lab can often be a good choice for a family with children, because the dog will be calmer than a puppy and will be less labor intensive for the parent(s) to care for. In a busy family, making time for all of a puppy's needs can be difficult.

Breed Truths

Some foods have a more profound effect on the Labrador Retriever's digestive system; however, it seems that even the most highly digestible, high-grade foods still produce copious amounts of fragrant flatulence. 'Nuff said on the subject.

If the adult Lab comes from a respected breed rescue, the dog's tolerance of children will already be known. Even with a proven kid-friendly dog, care will still need to be taken as the dog acclimates to your home, family members, and lifestyle.

With Other Pets

For the most part, Labradors are pretty good-natured and seem to get along well with other animals when raised with them. Some Labradors, however, even when raised with other pets at home, may show a higher drive to chase things. Be aware that the high-drive dog may chase pets in the home. Or, he may be fine in the home, but when the cat is in the yard, the chase is on. If this is the case with your Lab, you will need to make sure you can safely keep the pets separate in the home.

Breed Truths

The Lab is not a breed that challenges your leadership on a daily basis. However, to keep him from ever considering taking a leadership position, he has to know the rules, and the owner needs to provide kind and consistent guidance.

With Other Dogs

The Labrador Retriever is considered dog-friendly. This means the breed has a natural tendency to get along well with other dogs. Many factors can influence how dog-friendly a Lab is as an adult, however.

For example, if a puppy is separated from his littermates too early (before seven weeks), he is at risk for becoming more aggressive as an adult. Likewise, as a puppy grows, his experiences with other dogs count, too. If he is bullied or attacked by another dog, he might become more aggressive toward other dogs.

So there's no guarantee that a Labrador will be dog-friendly, but if you can ensure that the Lab's experiences with other dogs are fun and positive, he should remain dog-friendly throughout his life.

Labrador Retrievers and Learning the Rules

One of the true joys of owning a Labrador Retriever is in the breed's ability to learn. Regardless of your prior training experience, you *can* train a Labrador. The breed is very forgiving of what professional trainers call "handling errors," and most dogs are exceptionally eager to figure out what you want them to do.

The key to teaching a Lab the house rules is for everyone in the household to be *consistent* with the rules from day one. If you don't want your Lab to sleep on the bed with you, don't allow him to jump up some nights and kick him off other times. If you don't want him to beg at the dinner table, don't feed him scraps off your plate, and teach him to lie down on a mat during your mealtimes.

The Labrador Retriever is also an exceptional dog when it comes to training for both competitive and noncompetitive events. The breed has beaucoup energy and an intense focus on the handler, not to mention the willingness to perform an exercise over and over with unparalleled enthusiasm.

Helpful Hints

No breeder's lines are perfect or completely free of disease. A good breeder will be very upfront about this. She will show you where she is having problems and explain how she is working to resolve them.

This combination of traits (thanks again to generations of breeding for the perfect gundog!) makes the Labrador a candidate to participate in virtually any sport or activity you could possibly want. And don't rule out hunting events even if you don't hunt and/or your Lab was bred only as a companion: Most Labs (with training) can earn a working certificate or even entry-level hunting titles—and owners need not know how to fire a shotgun. (You *will* come away from the experience with a newfound awe of your dog's abilities—guaranteed!)

How a Lab Explores His World

There's a lot going on in the Lab's world. With a heightened sense of smell, the ability to hear higher frequencies than humans, and a completely different view of the world, the Labrador is bombarded with sensory information. In order to use the Lab's senses to your advantage, it's important to first understand how Labradors hear, see, and smell the world around them.

Helpful Hints

The Real Scoop

For a candid discussion on why most Labs *fail* in the home, talk to those who rescue Labs. A local or regional rescue near you can be found by searching the Lab rescue database on the LRC web site: *www.thelabradorclub.com/ subpages/searchrescue.php*

A dog's hearing is comparable to a human's in many ways; however, canines are able to hear higher frequencies that are inaudible to the human ear. That's why a silent whistle (higher frequency) can be used in training dogs and may also be why many Labs enjoy attacking the vacuum cleaner; it may be emitting a high frequency whine that we can't hear.

When it comes to vision, forget what you might have learned years ago. According to a recent Australian study dogs *do* see in color; they just can't see the color red very well. Additionally, the shape of a dog's eyes is now known to vary greatly between the breeds. *And,* perhaps the biggest surprise: there are two different types of retinas in dogs. Short nosed dogs have an "area centralis," or a sharply defined center vision with poorer peripheral vision. Longer nosed dogs, such as the Lab, have a "visual streak," in which the dog has sharp vision not only in front of him, but also far into his peripheral vision on both sides—possibly more than a 300 degree field of clear vision. The researchers in this study believe the presence of a visual streak explains why a dog, such as the Lab, is much more sensitive to movement and much more likely to hunt or chase a moving object.

Finally, there's the Lab's nose. The dog's greatest sense is his ability to smell, and the Labrador is a breed that uses this sense extensively in understanding his world. Dogs are believed to have roughly 225,000 olfactory receptors in their noses (contrasted with 9,000 in a human's nose). This enables a dog to detect substances in the low parts-per-billion range. The olfactory region (the part of the brain that deciphers what an animal smells) is also 40 times larger in the dog's brain than in the human's brain. Researchers believe that because of this, dogs are able to layer scents, much like humans can visually layer what they are seeing.

Although the Lab may not be able to physically smell any better than a Poodle, for example, the Lab's exceptional ability to alert to scents and the breed's excellent work ethic (he's happy working all day long) are characteristics that have made the breed a top choice for scent detection work.

Health Concerns

The Labrador Retriever is a relatively healthy breed, considering how popular it is. Unfortunately, the more popular a breed becomes, the more often people breed without making health one of their top priorities. As a result, this once robustly healthy breed has a higher incidence of some diseases among some populations of dogs. Puppy buyers need to be aware of this and choose their breeder and puppy carefully.

Diseases that are known (or strongly suspected) to have a genetic factor in the Labrador Retriever include allergies, canine hip dysplasia, elbow dysplasia, some forms of cancer, epilepsy, hypothyroidism, some skin disorders, heart disease, and several types of eye disease. (For more specific disease information and available tests, see Chapter 6: "Health and Nutrition.")

There are several conditions that are more common in Labradors as they age, in particular, fatty tumors, arthritis, and laryngeal paralysis. Fatty tumors (lipomas) are benign tumors, and though they can be unsightly, these tumors are only removed if they are uncomfortable. Arthritis may be a nuisance at first, but in some Labs it can become so advanced and painful as to require medications or sugery in order to provide relief. Laryngeal paralysis is frequently seen in elderly Labs and causes partial or full collapse of the larynx; serious cases of this condition can be fatal if left untreated, usually through surgery.

Though this is an abbreviated list of maladies that can strike the Labrador Retriever, there is a significant amount of disease in this breed. Dogs that are bred by conscientious breeders who not only test for genetic diseases but also track the prevalence of the various diseases in their lines (i.e., keeping in touch with puppy buyers and maintaining records of major health issues for each litter they've bred) have a significantly better chance of being free of serious, life-threatening diseases.

Putting It All Together

If you're looking for a terrific dog that is loyal, devoted, and generally up and ready for anything you are, the Labrador Retriever could be a great choice. If you're worried about the exceptionally high-energy puppy years—but still would love to have a Lab—adopting an adult dog may be the perfect solution for you.

In general, the breed is easy to train, and if his physical, mental, and emotional needs are met, he's usually a pretty easy keeper (though he can be a source of "constant motion" well into his senior years).

If you're still on the fence deciding whether the Labrador Retriever is for you, contact the Labrador Retriever Club of America

CHECKLIST

Is the Labrador Retriever the Dog for You?

You might be a Lab Lover *if* . . .

✔ you enjoy vacuuming;

✔ you don't mind playing fetch for *hours*;

✔ you get as excited as your dog does when you see a duck within range and in season;

✔ orange and camouflage take up a good portion of your wardrobe;

✔ you like taking your dog with you everywhere, and don't mind that he takes up the same amount of room in the car as all your children combined;

✔ you enjoy long walks on the beach, in the park, or in the neighborhood . . . several times a day;

✔ you think a wagging Lab tail is a good thing, because it serves double duty as a duster for those coffee and end tables you never use;

✔ you think dog training is FUN and can't get enough of it;

✔ when you find ten-foot trails of water dripped from the water bowl, you chalk it up to just another part of dog ownership;

✔ you're okay with bigger veterinary bills, higher boarding fees, greater pet food expenses, and more senior issues that come with owning a larger-breed dog, because what your Labrador gives you is priceless;

✔ you're looking for the most amazing canine companion you've ever experienced.

You might *not* be a Lab Lover *if* . . .

✔ you expect your butter to be free of dog hair;

✔ you believe a dog's place is in the backyard;

✔ you are a couch potato with no intention of changing your lifestyle;

✔ you think "eau de wet dog" is oh-you-better-be-gone dog smell;

✔ you have allergies (really) to dog dander;

✔ you expect your Lab to lie relaxed in front of the hearth just like the Labs in the paintings do;

✔ a fenced yard, in your mind, would not go with your landscaping, nor would the occasional deep hole or brown spots on your grass;

✔ the only time a dog rides in your car is when it's time for the annual veterinary exam;

✔ you don't like the colors black, yellow, or chocolate;

✔ your dog health care plan is as follows: If he's healthy, he can stay;

✔ you're acquiescing to a dog because your significant other is crazy about Labs;

✔ you're really a cat person.

(see "Resources," page 167 for complete contact information) and ask for referrals to breeders in your area. Call these breeders and ask questions about the breed and how well they adjust to family life.

Talk to owners who have recently experienced living with a young puppy and the issues they had to work through—there may be some problems you hadn't considered. And, take a look at how flexible *you* are in making lifestyle changes to meet your new dog's exercise, training, and care needs.

A great web site to check out is *www.Lab-Retriever.net*. You'll find discussions on all aspects of the Labrador from owners with all types of experience. Additional discussion lists can be found by searching *www.Yahoo.com* under member lists for Labrador Retrievers.

The Lab isn't the perfect dog for everyone—but he's a great dog for a lot of people. His good nature and ability to adapt to many different living situations (city, suburbs, and country) make him a widely popular choice as a family pet.

Communicating with Your Labrador Retriever

Voice After thousands of years as a domesticated animal, dogs in general are quite capable of interpreting the nature of what we are trying to say through our tone of voice, the volume with which we speak, and the inflection in our words. Regardless of what language you are speaking, dogs understand whether you are speaking to them in a happy, sad, or angry manner.

In addition to being able to pick up the subtleties of how we are saying our words, dogs are also believed to be capable of understanding hundreds of words. They can even pick out certain words when strung together in a sentence and make sense of what has been said.

With this said, it can appear at times, that the Labrador doesn't understand anything you've told him, particularly when you are scolding him. He continues to look up at you with soulful, brown eyes, and his tail never stops wagging. Sometimes called hard-headed, the Lab is, in reality, a breed that generally is not easily crushed by harsh verbal corrections. However, don't use this as an excuse to mistreat him. He will hear and understand what you are saying most quickly if you use positive, reward-based training techniques.

Hands Much of the way in which dogs communicate with each other is through body language. It is believed that dogs are very visual learners, the Lab included. What this means is that when you are training your dog, you will find that your puppy or adult Lab will excel at learning hand signals. You will be able to link a hand signal with a behavior quite easily. The advantage of teaching your Lab basic commands using hand signals is that you can show anyone of any age how to give the hand signals to the dog, and the Labby will understand what he is being told. With voice commands, a "Sit" may sound quite different coming from a high-pitched toddler than a deep-toned man. The Labby will pick up on these tonal differences and may possibly get confused. With hand signals, you will not find this confusion.

Facial Expressions If you watch your Lab as you are talking to him, it's very obvious that he has facial expressions. He will wrinkle his brow, relax and tighten his eyes, shift ear positions, open and close his mouth, etc. It's not just a saying—you can see what you Lab is thinking to some extent. Additionally, Labs can recognize people's facial expressions (remember, they're visual learners), and in fact, have been known to mimic a human's smile (which is not a dog behavior at all). When working to communicate with your dog, many trainers recommend combining appropriate facial expressions with rewards to help your Lab understand what you are training him to do. Smiling when you're pleased comes naturally to some people but is more difficult for others. (An angry look accompanied by a "no!" can get the message across much better than simply saying, "no!")

Body Movement

As noted previously, dogs communicate by using their bodies. Greeting behaviors among domestic dogs are highly ritualized, making them recognizable by all sizes, types, breeds, and mixes of dogs no matter where in the world they have been raised. Using your body to communicate your joy or displeasure can also help your Lab to understand what you are trying to communicate to him. Again, some owners have a harder time unleashing the inner thespian when training their dogs, and other owners sometimes are too demonstrative (which can overwhelm a timid dog). If your body language matches what you are trying to communicate, you will find that your Lab has an easier time understanding your message. Note: Threatening body language should never be used when working with dogs. Dominant actions do not make for good leaders; confident behavior and mannerisms *do* make for good leadership.

Scents

Labs can paint a picture in their minds from what they smell. The scent of urine on a telephone pole to the Lab is a detailed chapter on another dog: Male, intact, large breed, owner of the block or older male, neutered, looking for a good playmate. The Lab's ability to detect smells tells him much more about you than you can ever imagine. Dogs can detect changes in our chemical makeup and are capable of smelling a seizure thirty minutes before it occurs, and scenting out the early stages of several different types of cancer. It would be no surprise to many Lab owners if it was determined that Labs could actually scent out our mood changes. So although we can't purposefully communicate to our Labs using scents, the Lab may possibly have a greater understanding of our subconscious communications through the breed's incredible sense of smell.

Chapter Three

How to Choose a Labrador Retriever

Whether black, yellow, or chocolate, there's just something about that plush puppy coat, those dark eyes, sweet puppy licks, and the not-quite-so-coordinated full-tilt puppy play that makes Labrador Retriever puppies possibly the cutest things around. How do you choose? The best puppy for you will depend on a puppy's background and breeding, as well as your expectations for the Lab as an adult.

With Labs for sale virtually everywhere, it is important to know what you're looking for and what you're looking at before you even begin your search. Your new Lab will have the best chance of succeeding if he most closely fits both what you want in a dog (activity level, temperament, health, and looks) and what your lifestyle can afford as far as time and effort.

First, are you completely set on getting a puppy? Sure, they're cute, but they're also a lot of work for their first, oh, three or four *years* in the home. Contrast this with an adult dog that may already know a few commands, is (mostly) house trained, and is just looking for a family to love. The average life span of a Labrador Retriever is 10 to 12 years; however, healthy Labs can live even longer, so adopting a six- or seven-year-old healthy dog can mean many wonderful years together. Lots of terrific young adult dogs are given up to shelters and rescues all the time, so if you're not completely set on purchasing a puppy, you might want to weigh the pros and cons of both purchasing a puppy and adopting a dog.

What's in a Line?

When looking for a Labrador Retriever breeder, you will most likely hear a lot of different terms used to describe the breeding or lines behind a given litter of puppies. Breeding for a purpose makes the potential greater for a puppy to have certain instincts and conformation; however, keep in mind that every puppy is an individual. Therefore, a puppy bred for hunting may turn out to have little hunting instinct, and it is possible for a show-bred pup from untested parents (hunting instincts unknown) to turn out to be an extraordinary hunter.

Here's a short list of what these different terms mean—not only to the potential characteristics of the puppy from these lines, but also how this could translate in the home.

Field Lines

Historically, *all* Labrador Retrievers come from field (or hunting) lines. Today, however, "field" lines means that a puppy's parents are either actively competing in field trials or hunt tests, and/or are used regularly as a personal hunting dog. In other words, Labradors from field lines are bred specifically for strong hunting instincts.

As a result, field lines are associated with intense retrieving instincts (they carry *everything*), higher energy levels (not to be confused with hyperactivity, which is a high energy level without *focus*), and lots of endurance. These dogs *may* be a bit taller and more slender with a less blocky head and a sleeker coat than other lines of Labs; *however, this is not always the case*. A field-bred Lab may be very close to the breed standard, or he could be bred more with hunting drives and function in mind.

Breeders who compete in field trials, hunt tests, and other dog sports are conscientious about health testing and breeding for temperament. Well-bred Labs from field lines will be healthy and have good temperaments.

For the Owner If you are sedentary or are seeking a "hearth" dog that will lie quietly by the fireplace, purchasing a puppy from true field lines could be disastrous if you're not willing to change your lifestyle immediately. Field-bred Labrador Retrievers are typically of such extraordinary energy and have such intense drives that puppies from these lines must have a home in which the owner is willing to become involved in training for hunt tests *or* another activity that meets this dog's needs, such as agility, tracking, or search and rescue. Can the field-bred Labrador do well in a pet home? Certainly, but only if the family is willing and able to keep up with this high-paced, driven dog. Are there exceptions to the rule (a less-demanding, field-bred dog)? Absolutely, but determining which pup in a litter *might* be less demanding can be difficult at such a young age.

Breed Truths

Heights and weights can vary widely within the breed, with some dogs barely weighing in at 50 pounds and others topping the scales at 100. The preferred height (per the breed standard) is 22½ to 24½ inches for males and 21½ to 23½ inches for females. The preferred weight is 65 to 80 pounds for males and 55 to 70 pounds for females.

Show Lines

"Show" Labradors are bred to most closely conform to the breed standard and are absolutely gorgeous. Show Labs *may* appear a bit sturdier (but they aren't fat!) and have less leg than a field dog. Show Labs may also have wider skulls and shorter muzzles, giving the appearance of a larger, blockier head. Many of these dogs retain solid hunting characteristics, and frequently, breeders will train and test for Working Certificates and hunt test titles to make sure their lines retain the qualities necessary for a good retriever. In addition, Labs that are bred for conformation are also health tested and bred for the classic Lab temperament most pet owners are seeking.

For the Owner Labs from show lines still have a lot of energy (particularly as puppies and young adults); however, they are generally considered calmer and less challenging to keep occupied than their field counterparts. Most puppies in a litter bred for show are sold to pet homes, as much as 80 percent of a litter. Purchasing a pup from show lines and from

BE PREPARED! Top 10 Benefits of Adopting an Adult

Reason #10: Health Problems Are Identified. Most adults available for adoption are old enough that if they have an inherited, chronic, or potentially life-threatening illness it will most likely be evident. If a dog *does* have an illness, you'll know the cost of his treatment and any limitations he might have before choosing to adopt him.

Reason #9: Temperament Is Known. Yes, environment does play a role in the development of a puppy's temperament. And yes, it is true that with the adult dog you can't go back in time and change what has happened to him. With an adult Lab, however, you can get a clear picture about how he's weathered the storm. In short, if he's got a great temperament despite neglect and mistreatment, you've got a diamond in the rough that will only sparkle more when he's got a loving home.

Reason #8: What You See Is *Really* What You Get! Ever heard of the Lab puppy with small paws that grew into a 100-pound buster (with comparatively small paws)? If you adopt an adult, you'll know his full, adult size, coat type, coloring, head shape, body type—you name it. No surprises here!

Reason #7: Better Bladder Control. If the rescued Lab hasn't already been house trained by the time you adopt him, it won't take you very long to teach him. An adult can hold *eons* longer than an eight-week-old pup, and this goes a long way in teaching the ropes of house training—especially if you work.

Reason #6: Routine Veterinary Care Complete. Most Lab rescues and shelters fully vaccinate dogs before adoption. If altering isn't included in the adoption fee, it is usually offered at a much reduced rate.

Reason #5: The Price Is Right! Speaking of money . . . A rescued Lab costs a *fraction* of the cost of a puppy.

Reason #4: Less Destruction. Most adult dogs are beyond the heavy chewing, shredding, nipping, über-mouthy stage. Chances are he'll still pick up "carryable" things around the house—so they'll be slobbery, but they're more likely to be in one piece.

Reason #3: Time to Relax. With a little age comes a little tranquility. The adult Lab is not nearly as rambunctious and active as a puppy, nor are his demands for strenuous exercise as high. Activity levels vary among adult Labs just as they do with pups; however, you'll know *exactly* what your adult Labby's exercise demands will be before you bring him home.

Reason #2: Ready to Go. There's no waiting with the adopted Labrador for a puppy vaccination series to be completed—he's ready to go on walks, swim, participate in play groups, take a training class (or two or three) *for fun*, and visit with friends.

Reason #1: The Best Reason of All—The Lab Picks YOU!!! Perhaps the greatest advantage to adopting an adult dog is that the process allows *the dog* to pick whom he wants as his owner. When a dog picks the person he wants as his "person" (and the feeling is mutual), it's always a win-win situation.

a breeder who can help guide your selection toward the puppy that is most likely to meet your expectations can help make sure the right pup goes in the right home.

Working Lines

Many government, nonprofit, and private-sector organizations involved with scent detection or service dogs have established their own Labrador Retriever breeding programs. The purpose of these programs is to provide dogs that are most likely to have the health, temperament, and special skill sets that their individual programs require. Working-dog programs usually produce Labs with a good work ethic (comfortable being on the job for ten or more hours at a time), as well as good health and rock-solid temperaments. Adhering to the breed standard for conformation is not of great importance for a working Lab, so Labs from these programs will have functional conformation (a build that best suits the dog's work), but may not look like the Labs you find in the conformation ring. Labs from working programs become available to the general public when a dog does not make the cut during one of the stages of his training.

BE PREPARED! Top 10 Benefits of Purchasing a Puppy

Reason #10: Puppies Are Cute. There's no denying that holding a Lab puppy is one of the most wonderful feelings in life. Keep in mind that puppies are cute for a reason . . . . If they weren't so adorable, you wouldn't be likely to tolerate all the challenges of owning a young dog.

Reason #9: You Get to Pick. Well, sort of. You get to pick your breeder and the litter of puppies; however, when picking the actual puppy, you may be more limited. A top-notch breeder's puppies are in demand, and many will already have been selected for other owners. If you've found a great breeder, however, he or she will be able to pinpoint the best potential puppy or puppies *for you* in a litter.

Reason #8: You Inherit a Mentor. A reputable breeder is incredibly knowledgeable about the breed and *wants* his or her puppies to do well in their new homes. A puppy's breeder will be able to help you through all the rough patches with your pup and raise him to be a great companion.

Reason #7: The Pup Doesn't Come with Baggage. Adult dogs have been around for a little while, and much of their habits, phobias, and behaviors are based on their past life experiences. A puppy has only the baggage you pack for him.

Reason #6: Opportunity to Work on Your Sleep-deprivation Skills. This could be a valuable skill for someone . . . somewhere . . . maybe?

Reason #5: You Get to Raise Him "Right." Raising a puppy is a big responsibility. You can control his learning environment, ensuring that he doesn't have any frightening experiences and that he learns through positive experience.

Reason #4: Early Training for Performance Events Can Be Started . . . Early. A dog's performance as an adult in some competitive (and noncompetitive) events can be heightened by working with basic skills when a dog is a puppy.

Reason #3: Get Rid of Clutter Without Having a Yard Sale. Lab puppies are adept at finding anything that is loose (and often things that aren't). If you don't find these items before your puppy does, it will be orally sampled (chewed, chunked, and swallowed—which is extremely dangerous for the puppy).

Reason #2: Puppies Often Can Be More Easily Added to a Multi-pet, Multi-species Home. Older, adult dogs may be more accepting of a puppy than of another adult dog. Also, puppies raised with members of different species, such as cats, house rabbits, birds, etc., *may* accept these other creatures as family members. (Note: This does not ensure that the puppy won't try to retrieve these other family members . . . .)

Reason #1: You Get to See Him Grow Up. The puppy months go by very quickly and are truly a once-in-a-lifetime event for both dog and owner. Raising a puppy is certainly hard work, but there are many benefits that go along with this labor of love.

For the Owner "Washouts" from working programs are typically young adults, so you'll know exactly what you're getting. Young Labs from working programs know basic obedience commands and are house trained. The Labs in these programs are well socialized, too. If you are considering adopting a dog from one of these programs, be sure to find out *why* a dog is being offered for adoption. The placement services for working-dog programs are generally quite sophisticated and do an excellent job of determining if a dog that is being pulled from their program will be suitable for your lifestyle.

Companion-bred Labs

This is a gentler term for Labs that have been bred for no particular reason. (Other names could include backyard bred, or, depending on the source, a puppy-mill product.) These Labs are not bred with form or function in mind and are often the source of many hereditary illnesses, because parents of these pups are rarely tested or screened for any diseases.

Fun Facts

A "dual champion" dog is one that has been awarded a field trial championship (FCh) for his retrieving abilities, and a show championship (Ch) for his conformation to the breed standard.

Most important, a companion-bred Lab is not a guarantee of the calm, steady temperament that is the hallmark of this breed; quirky and unstable temperaments are becoming increasingly common among poorly bred dogs, and the Lab is no exception.

For the Owner Steer clear of dogs that aren't bred for a purpose by a reputable breeder. Health and temperament are uncertain with these dogs, and hyperactivity (high energy *without focus*) is more prevalent.

Breeders Compared

The key to finding a great Labrador Retriever puppy, one that meets your every expectation as to what a good Lab should be, is finding a great breeder. But how do you know who's naughty and who's nice (and responsible and knowledgeable and has great dogs?)

First, reputable, knowledgeable breeders are involved somehow, some way, in the sport of dogs. They could be very involved in the show ring with some involvement in the hunting world, possibly through hunt tests or working certificates. Or, their breeding program could be focused primarily on the hunting arena, and their efforts are recorded with field trial titles, hunt test titles, and scores of solid gundogs working in the field with their owners.

Breed Truths

Well-bred Labs do not cost more in the long run. The potential for costly health problems with a poorly bred Lab is so great that the slightly higher cost of a well-bred pup easily pays for itself within the first few years of ownership.

If a Labrador Retriever breeder is *not* involved in some aspect of the dog fancy—show or field—that should be a red flag to any potential puppy buyer. It is only by working with these dogs that a person can have a true appreciation for what is correct in the breed and what is not.

Another red flag is if the breeder sells his or her puppies only by listing them in newspapers or all-breed magazines. Typically, reputable breeders use word of mouth to sell their litters or promote upcoming litters in specialty publications that are targeted directly for Labrador Retriever owners, breeders, trainers, and exhibitors, such as the *LRC Newsletter*, *The Labrador Quarterly*, and *Retriever News*.

Finding a Good Breeder

One of the best ways to find a good Labrador Retriever breeder in your area is to start at the top—with one of the national breed clubs. The Labrador Retriever Club, Inc. (AKC), the National Labrador Retriever Club (FCI), and the United Labrador Retriever Association (United Kennel Club) offer breeder referral services for interested puppy buyers. When you contact the club, you will be put in touch with someone in your area.

This breeder may or may not have puppies available at that moment, but after talking with you and finding out more clearly what type

FYI: Who's Who in Breeding

	Show Breeder	Field Breeder	Pet Breeder	Puppy Mill
Member of national breed club	Yes	Yes	No	No
Member of local/regional breed club	Usually	Possibly	No	No
Member of one or more field/hunting clubs	Possibly	Yes	No	No
Participant in AKC shows	Yes	Possibly*	No	No
Participant in field trials	Possibly	Yes	No	No
Participant in hunt tests	Frequently	Yes	No	No
Tests for a variety of health issues before breeding and provides proof of testing	Yes	Yes	No	No
Breeds only to improve the breed	Yes	Yes	No	No
Screens puppy buyers for suitability with breed	Yes	Yes	No	No
If something doesn't work out, requires owner to return Lab or allows breeder to help owner place dog in new home	Yes	Yes	No	No
Contract	Yes	Yes	No	Yes, but the terms protect the seller, not the buyer
Health guarantee	Yes	Yes	No	Yes, but watch out for the terms

*Many puppies are sold to competitive obedience and agility homes.

of lifestyle you have and what kinds of dog activities you're interested in, he or she will be able to direct you to someone who does have puppies (or will have puppies in the near future).

Most all-breed clubs have several members who are involved in Labrador Retrievers. A listing of all-breed clubs that are affiliated with the AKC are listed on the AKC's Web site and can be searched by area of the country.

Check out obedience and agility clubs. Labradors are fun dogs to train and are frequently seen at obedience and agility clubs. Usually, owners are more than pleased to tell you where they purchased their dogs and to recommend a breeder.

BE PREPARED! Reading Between the Lines

Everyone is on the Internet; however, slick Web sites give nonreputable breeders the opportunity to appear authentic. They may say the right things (these folks read the "how to buy a puppy" articles, too), but if you look closely, you can usually read between the lines and easily spot which people are high-quality Lab breeders and which are merely posers.

Web Site Red Flags	What This Might Mean
Dogs listed by first names only	The dogs don't have any titles either in the field or show ring. (High-quality breeders are proud of their dogs' accomplishments and will list their dogs' entire names, complete with titles earned.)
No national or regional club affiliations noted on Web site	The breeder is not really that involved with any aspect of the breed
Accepts all major credit cards	The seller is broadcasting that he or she is more interested in making a sale than making sure the puppy is the right fit for his new family
Ships anywhere in the United States or world	It would be very difficult for a breeder to match the right puppy to you and your family without meeting you
Limited or no health tests listed for parents of litters; or the breeder "explains" why health testing isn't necessary (in his or her mind)	You can't have healthy puppies if you don't have healthy parents
Sells multiple breeds	Reputable breeders *rarely* specialize in more than one breed; puppy mills and those trying to make a buck sell several different kinds of breeds

Web Tip: Run a search on the seller's name, kennel name, and URL. Often, a Web site may appear to be selling one breed but a search reveals that the person simply has a separate Web site set up for each breed he or she is selling.

At the Shows . . .

Another way to locate a high-quality breeder is to attend a dog show. Here you can sit ringside and watch the Labrador Retriever classes. When judging has finished, talk to the handlers of the dogs you are interested in. Or, walk back to where the RVs and exhibitor vehicles are parked. You'll see Labbies in exercise pens and crates in the shade with owners or handlers waiting for their next ring time. This is a nice, relaxed time to talk to people about their dogs. Be sure to purchase a catalog at dog shows. These catalogs not only list information on all entered dogs, but also provide contact information for the dogs' owners.

In the Field . . .

If you're more interested in a dog with the potential to compete in field trials, partici-pate in hunt tests, or serve as a personal hunting companion, it's best to find a breeder at a field trial or hunt test in your area. (To find a schedule of events, see Chapter 10 for a listing of organizations and contact information.)

At retriever trials and tests, you will be able to see the dogs and handlers compet-ing from an area set up as a "gallery" for observers to watch. Take notes; you will get a lot of helpful advice and contact information from a range of owners, handlers, trainers, and family members sitting in the gallery.

Helpful Hints

Regional and local Labrador Retriever clubs are also good sources for high-quality breeders, as are national, regional, and local hunt clubs. To find local clubs search the various national sanc-tioning organizations for listings of affiliate clubs.

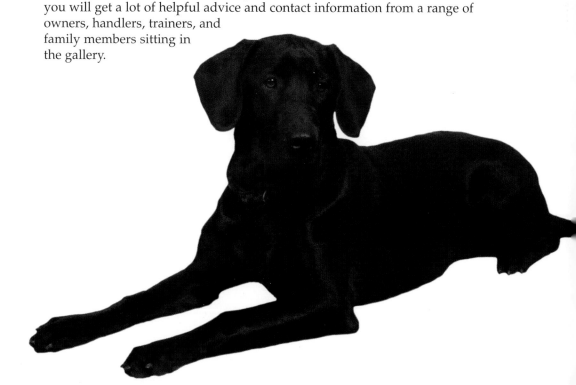

Titles are a source of pride for breeders and owners alike and show a dog's accomplishments. Your puppy's pedigree will reflect three generations of Labradors before him and all that they've achieved. Here's a brief breakdown of what some of the titles you might see mean.

Before the Dog's Name:

CH	Champion (show)
FC	Field Champion (Field Trial)
Dual CH	Conformation and Field Champion
AFC	Amateur Field Champion (Field Trial champion handled by an amateur)
NFC	National Field Champion (winner of the National Field Trial)
HR	Hunting Retriever (intermediate level, Hunting Retriever Club)
HRCH	Hunting Retriever Champion
GRHRCH	Grand Hunting Retriever Champion
MHR	Master Hunter Retriever
GMHR	Grand Master Hunter Retreiver

After the Dog's Name:

WC	Working Certificate (basic retriever skills, awarded by LRC)
JH	Junior Hunter (entry level, hunt tests)
SH	Senior Hunter
MH	Master Hunter
CD	Companion Dog (entry level, obedience)
CDX	Companion Dog Excellent
UD	Utility Dog
NA	Novice Agility (AKC)
OA	Open Agility
AX	Agility Excellent

Health Screenings and Tests

Health, health, health. It's the one thing that every book and article covers, but when it comes right down to it, a puppy's potential health problems as an adult are something very few puppy buyers really stop to consider. And who can really blame them? Who wants to think about crippling, chronic, and/or fatal diseases when you're looking at beautiful, bright-eyed puppies?

The Tests

There are certain tests that absolutely should be performed before breeding dogs, tests that every puppy's parents should have. In addition, several

FYI: What's a CHIC number?

If a Labrador Retriever has a "CHIC" number, that means that the dog's breeder tested the dog for hip dysplasia, elbow dysplasia, and eye disorders and has registered the results with the Canine Health Information Center (CHIC). (Testing for Centronuclear Myopathy (CNM), also known as hereditary myopathy or "Labrador Retriever Myopathy" is optional.) The dog must have a permanent form of identification (e.g., tattoo, microchip), too. A CHIC number *does not* mean the dog is clear of disease; it *does* mean that the tests were performed, and the results have been registered and made available to the public to review.

other genetic tests are currently considered "optional" for Labradors but are highly recommended.

Hip Dysplasia This test cannot be certified unless a dog is two years of age (or older) and records the potential for disease in a joint based on the looseness of the fit. (See "Hip Dysplasia," page 90.) The results are recorded with the Orthopedic Foundation of America (OFA) and the results *are searchable*. At a minimum, parents of the puppies should be "OFA-ed," but in a perfect world, parents, grandparents, and great-grandparents would all be certified clear of the disease.

Elbow Dysplasia As with hip dysplasia, the potential for elbow dysplasia is measured when the Lab is one to two years of age and the results are recorded with OFA. Again, at least one generation but preferably more should be clear of this disease.

C.E.R.F. When a breeder says a dog's eyes have been "CERF-ed," he or she is describing an annual certification by the Canine Eye Registry Foundation that a veterinary board-certified ophthalmologist has examined a dog's eyes. You want to make sure that the exam is current (performed *annually*) and that the results find the dogs' eyes clear of hereditary eye disease.

Other Tests

These DNA-based tests are not required by the Labrador Retriever Club (for its members); however, more breeders are using these tests to ensure that they know whether their breeding dogs are carriers or clear of these diseases. As researchers continue to work on genetics-based diseases and tests, more conditions that plague the breed will become available for testing.

CAUTION

Breeders have produced false "certifications" to unsuspecting buyers. If there's any doubt, write the numbers of the certification down and check with the certifying organization.

FYI: Does Color Count?

Some people prefer black, swearing they're the smartest and shed the least; others love yellow Labs, sometimes agreeing that the shed rate can be greater, but there's no lack of brain power with these dogs and there's the added benefit of having a wide range of shades within the yellow coat color (from fox red to a pale cream). And, some folks are definite chocolate lovers, even though there seems to be a lingering bit of bias against the color (some hunters claim that chocolates are more stubborn, less birdy, and more difficult to train). Take any color criticisms with a grain of salt: A dog's temperament and drives are more a product of his parents' genetics than a link to a specific color!

Progressive Retinal Atrophy (PRA) A DNA test is available to confirm not only if a Labrador has this eye disorder (for more information, see "PRA," page 93) but also if a dog is a carrier (and symptom-free) or genetically free of the disease.

Exercise-induced Collapse (EIC) This disorder appears both in field and show lines of Labrador Retrievers (for more information, see "EIC," page 92). A genetic test is available to determine if a dog has the disorder, is a carrier, or is clear of the disease.

Centronuclear Myopathy (CNM1) Also called Labrador muscular Myopathy, CNM is a muscle weakness disease that can be tested through a DNA-based test, similar to those for PRA and EIC.

Choosing the Puppy

You've found a great breeder; you're looking at a litter of ten bright-eyed puppies that are all clamoring for your attention. How do you decide? Here are a few guidelines to help you in your search.

1. **What are the pup's parents like?** You may not be able to see the stud, but you will be able to see the mother. (It's not uncommon for the stud dog *not* to be on the premises; the female may have been shipped to be bred or been artificially inseminated.) If you can meet with one or both parents of the litter, observe their basic temperaments. You want to see friendly, outgoing, and healthy-appearing dogs.
2. **Visit the puppies more than once, at different times.** Multiple visits help you get a better picture of what each pup is really like. Depending on when the pups have eaten, whether they're due for a nap, or whether it's time for play, the puppies may act quite differently each time you visit. One visit they may appear to be quiet, calm, and perfect little hearth dogs. (They've just been fed and it's time for a nap.) Come back the next morning when they've just woken up

from their nap, and you'll see a blur of fur and wild, high-paced, physical play.

3. **Watch the puppies interact with each other.** Some puppies play nicely, others are a little pushier, and still others may not like to play quite as hard. What's important to observe is how the pups react to each other: If one puppy yelps, does the "offending" puppy recognize his mistake and play more gently, or does he keep pushing?

4. **Who is interested in you?** When you say, "Puppy, puppy, puppy!" which pup (or puppies) comes running to you to see what's going on and which puppies completely ignore you? Try walking away from the puppy pack and see who follows you. Who's curious?

5. **Maybe *not* the middle one . . .** The old advice used to be to steer clear of the pushiest puppy and the quietest puppy and go for one of the "pups in the middle." The thought here was to avoid picking the dominant and shy puppies in a litter, which would be more difficult to raise. But here's the exception to this: What if the entire litter is full of drive, strong willed, and athletic? In this litter, the polite puppy may have been the pushy pup in another litter. Or, the most playful and persistent puppy in a litter of more timid pups may have

Breed Truths

Male or Female?

Many people think that females are sweeter, gentler dogs. There are always exceptions; however, in general, females actually tend to be a bit more independent than males. Looking for the most affectionate, doting Lab? Many Lab owners swear that a neutered male is the ticket.

PERSONALITY POINTERS
Puppy Aptitude Testing

There are many variations of puppy aptitude tests circulating among members of the dog world, and one thing that can be said for them is that none are tremendously accurate. What the following tests *can* do is give you an idea about how easy or challenging your puppy might be to work with when teaching the rules of the house and light obedience skills.

Test	How You Test	What You're Looking For
Boldness	Place an open cardboard box on the floor near the puppies	A puppy that shows curiosity without aggression (barking) or timidity (tail down, crouching toward the box)
Trust	Gently interlock fingers under a puppy's belly and just barely lift him from the floor; his paws should be just off the floor	A puppy that is relatively relaxed and doesn't put up a fuss, wriggle hard, or try to bite to be put back down immediately
Reactivity	Stand a couple of yards away from the puppies and smack two blocks of wood together to make a loud noise	It's okay for the puppies to jump, but look for which puppies react afterward with curiosity
Retrieving Instinct	Toss a ball to each of the puppies	The puppy that runs after the ball, picks it up, *and brings it back to you*
Companion Potential	Call the pup over to you while sitting on the floor	Lots of excited puppy kisses

been a quiet puppy in a pushy litter. Working with an experienced breeder helps a lot in a situation such as this; he or she will recognize the range of temperaments and activity levels within the litter and know where each pup falls, helping you to make the best choice.

6. **Bring an experienced Lab person with you.** If you're not working with a really reputable breeder and you're uncertain about what you're looking at in a litter, bring along someone who really knows Labrador Retrievers or at least is really familiar with sporting-breed dogs—a trainer, a handler, or a behaviorist. The fee that a professional may charge for this service can easily outweigh the frustration and heartache of making the wrong choice. To find a professional trainer, handler, or behaviorist who can help you select a puppy, see "Behavior/Training" on page 169 in the "Resources" chapter.

Adopting the Adult Labrador Retriever

If you're considering adopting an adult Labrador, you're in luck. You'll have literally scores of dogs to choose from. The hard part will be deciding which dog is right for you. Warning: They will almost always want to come home with *you*.

Rescues, Shelters, and Other Facilities Compared

Depending on where you select your Labrador from, you may have access to an amazing array of services (from complete veterinary workups to temperament testing and "basic training") or you may be left pretty much on your own when selecting and evaluating a dog.

The following are some of the most commonly seen differences between organizations that offer dogs up for adoption.

Lab Rescue Dogs that are in Lab rescue have had a complete veterinary exam, are altered, have been temperament tested, are house trained (or close to it), are crate trained (content to rest in a crate when asked), know a few basic commands, and are thoroughly evaluated for their acceptance of other dogs, kids, small children,

Helpful Hints

The Labrador Retriever Club, Inc. maintains a searchable network of local and regional Labrador Rescues on their Web site: *www.thelabradorclub.com*. A Google search with "Lab Rescue" and your area will produce contact information, too.

and often, when possible, cats. The dogs are raised in a home environment, so they are acclimated to life as house dogs.

Shelters The level of services and the quality of the shelter facility depends largely on the charity of those living in the surrounding community. A growing number of nonprofit organizations offer an incredible assortment of services, including on-staff animal behaviorists and post-adoption reduced-rate veterinary services and training classes.

The dogs are kept in kennels, but efforts are made to determine how a dog might adapt to home life, and to test to see how the dog does with other dogs and cats. Depending on what your local shelter offers, you may have a full-service facility or one that isn't able to provide as many services.

Municipally Run "Pounds" or Animal Control This facility is composed primarily of dogs that are picked up as strays—dogs that were dropped off as unwanted by their owners. Dogs are kept in kennels, and other than treatment for fleas and ticks, not much else is usually provided for the animals (though this varies with the facility). Usually, it's a short stay for a dog in these facilities—unless a local breed rescue or shelter "springs" the animal from the facility.

The Adoption Process

If you're adopting a dog from a local pound or animal control center, the application process is usually fairly simple. You will need to be 21 years old

Elle Wilmer

and able to show proof of residence. Fees are minimal, with $40 to $60 being fairly standard; however, as these facilities improve their services, the adoption fee may be higher.

At a non-profit shelter, in addition to the above requirements, you will be asked to fill out a questionnaire, and will be informally interviewed by a staff member at the facility. At this point, you will be assisted in meeting different dogs. If you find a dog you're interested in, the facility will ask that the rest of your family members meet the dog to make sure that everyone gets along. If you have one or more dogs at home, you'll be asked to bring your current dog to the shelter, where a staff member will oversee the initial introduction to the potential new dog.

If you're adopting from a Lab rescue, you will go through all the steps listed above *and* someone will come to your home and do a "home check" before you're allowed to adopt a Labby. This step is to confirm that the adopter has been truthful about his or her living situation, *and* if the adopter has any potentially challenging issues, the experienced rescue volunteer can help the individual by giving him or her suggestions or innovative solutions.

What to Expect

Rescued Labs are terrific. You'll know immediately when you've found the right dog because he'll tell you. These dogs are ready and willing to bond with their new owners and seem to be particularly grateful to have a warm, loving home. It is important, however, to take things slowly with a rescued Lab. It takes time to form a solid bond between owner and dog, and most important, the new owner will need to earn the Lab's trust.

Once you've got the dog's trust, you have his heart—the greatest gift a Lab can give a person.

Chapter Four

Caring for a New Labrador Retriever

Your new puppy or rescued adult dog is finally home. It's a very exciting time for everyone, including the Labrador. The first day is filled with fun and then night comes and . . . Hold on! It can't be bedtime yet. Your new Lab still wants to have fun. This chapter will help you acclimate your puppy or rescued adult to home life as quickly and with as little drama as possible.

Preparing for Your Lab's Arrival

The first thing you want to do, if you haven't already, is make your home and yard safe for your new Lab. Keep in mind that it is "classic Lab" to want to pick up everything and chew on it. Nothing within reach of a puppy is safe from a little bit of sampling. Anything that fits in an adult dog's mouth will be carried.

The problem is more than just slobber and teeth marks in everything in your home; Labs will swallow chunks of whatever they are chewing. (Who knows? It *might* be edible!) If you've Lab-proofed your home and yard, the worst you'll ever experience is Technicolor, crayon-laced feces. If you've missed something, your Labby might need emergency surgery to save his life.

Make sure you have all needed items at hand before you bring your new Lab home. Be sure to purchase the food recommended by the breeder or shelter, bowls, toys, collars, and leashes. If you will be crate training your Lab, be sure to purchase one that is large enough for him to comfortably move around in. And, of course, don't forget soft cozy bedding.

Breed Truths

Adopted adult dogs that haven't had any home experience may go through a second puppyhood and behave much like a young pup might. Just be prepared for inquisitive chewing, regardless of your new Lab's age.

Labrador Retriever Supplies

Here's a list of what you'll need before your Lab puppy or rescued adult comes home.

Food Find out what kind of food the breeder or shelter has been feeding your Lab and purchase the exact same food. Sudden changes in food can cause gastrointestinal upset—not something you want on your Labby's first day home!

Bowls Purchase bowls for both food and water. Weighted bowls or those that don't tip over easily (or aren't easily picked up and carried) are good choices.

Crate This should be big enough to stand up, turn around, and lie down in. Puppies will go through two sizes or more as they grow. Plastic crates are the least expensive; however, sturdy, collapsible wire crates are also good choices.

Bedding Your new Labby will need something soft to curl up on that fits the bottom of the crate. Be careful not to give a young puppy plush bedding until he's gotten beyond the shredding-and-eating bedding stage, which can be lethal.

Collar A plain, quick-release snap collar or a buckle collar are good choices. It doesn't have to be fancy, but something you can hang an identification tag on and snap a leash to will work fine.

Leash A four-foot leash is a good length for Labs that don't know leash manners. (They can graduate to a six-foot leash when they're better behaved.) For puppies, choose a thin leash with a small clip; there's nothing worse than a huge clip banging the puppy in the head when you're trying to teach him leash manners!

CHECKLIST

Lab-proofing

Inside

✔ Cover all electrical cords, including stereo and computer wiring.

✔ Clear coffee table of trinkets: This is as much for chewing as for tail sweeping by larger dogs.

✔ Shut doors to bathrooms (some Labs love to drink from the toilet and some have toilet paper fetishes).

✔ Remove all rodenticides, ant traps, roach traps, and other poisons.

✔ Use rubber bands to shut or to secure cabinet drawers under sinks, to prevent access to cleaning supplies.

✔ Purchase child latches for drawers.

✔ Put garbage cans behind closed doors; trash cans should also be removed until it is determined whether the Lab enjoys shredding paper.

✔ Put prescriptions, vitamins, and supplements behind cabinet doors; the containers are *not* Lab-proof!

✔ Pick up miscellaneous loose items off the floor—coins, socks, underwear, action heroes, shoes, newspapers, magazines, etc. If it's on the floor, it's fair game for your Lab to chew.

Outside

✔ Walk the fence and check for loose boards or possible escape holes in chain-link fencing.

✔ Review plantings in your yard for poisonous or toxic plants (see *www.aspca.org* under "Animal Poison Control Center" for a complete listing).

✔ Replace toxic mulches, such as those made from cocoa (some dogs also get quite ill from red-dyed mulches).

✔ Watch decorative pebbles and stones; some Labbies find these great to chew and swallow.

✔ Remove snail and slug baits; these are poisonous to dogs.

✔ Be cautious with weed killers; many are highly toxic and others are more neutral only when completely dry.

✔ Walk around the foundation of your home and look for any potential crawl holes (or critter holes) that might be too enticing for your Lab to ignore.

✔ If you have a deck, make sure there is lattice preventing your puppy from running underneath it—unless you don't mind crawling under to rescue him.

✔ Clear brambles and debris that could injure a puppy or adult dog, and keep the grass mowed short to make it less favorable for flea infestations.

Toys Gotta have a few toys for the new dog. Make sure that any toys you purchase cannot be shredded, broken, chomped in pieces, and/or swallowed. So, stay away from stuffed toys, toys made from thin latex or vinyl that's easily shredded, and chew bones made of rawhide. Safe toys include size-appropriate Kong toys (i.e., don't buy a toy-dog-sized Kong for an adult Lab, because he'll ingest it without chewing), Nylabone puppy and adult chew toys, and the Almost Indestructible Ball, to name a few varieties to get you started shopping.

House Training Supplies Your pup *will* have accidents, so be ready to clean them up from day one (For a supply list, see "House training Made Easy," page 62.)

The First Day

The first day your puppy or rescued adult comes home should be all about the Lab. Puppy parties are the latest thing; however, refrain from inviting tons of friends and neighbors over to see your new, wonderful companion. Between your home, yard, and family, the Lab will have enough new things to explore, people to meet, and trouble to get into. You'll have your hands full!

Enjoy your first day (or days) with your new puppy. Be sure to give him plenty of time to sleep and rest. Encourage him to eat on a regular schedule. And make sure he knows where his crate, bed, and water are.

Puppy's First Night

It used to be common advice to new puppy owners to let their puppies cry themselves to sleep in their crates. It also used to be common advice to new mothers to let their babies cry in their cribs. Now we know that this may not be the best advice.

When it comes to a puppy, his night crying could be caused by a combination of loneliness, cold (there's no warm puppy pile!), fear of a new place, a need to relieve himself, and hunger.

Until your puppy is house trained, you can't expect them to sleep in a *big* bed and be accident-free. So, start off with a comfy crate kept close to your bed. To help make your Lab's crate more comfortable and inviting, try these tips.

- Layer the crate with newspapers and add a thick layer of shredded papers that the pup can snuggle into.
- Wrap a hot-water bottle in a towel and place it in the crate with the pup.
- Add a snuggly blanket, but watch to make sure the puppy doesn't shred it (and ingest it).

- Spray D.A.P. (Dog Appeasing Pheromone) in the crate; this compound simulates the hormone that nursing dogs emit and is a source of comfort for Labs of *all ages*.
- Offer a safe chew toy to keep the pup occupied; it's similar in effect to a pacifier for infants and often can help a pup go to sleep.
- Place the crate next to your bed so that you can reach down and comfort your pup as needed. Some owners will spend the night on the floor with the pup in the crate, just so the puppy knows someone is right next to him.

Acclimating to the Crate

Helpful Hints

Getting a puppy or adult dog comfortable with a crate is important for both house training and keeping the level of Lab destruction (good intentions; bad results) lower in the home. It's also helpful in keeping your Labby *safe*: If you can't supervise him 24/7, at least you know he's contained when you can't be watching him.

Adult dogs bond very quickly, but it does take some time to build up a dog's trust in you. Go slowly. Help him with the house rules in a positive manner and allow him to adjust on his own time frame.

Of course, for a crate to be helpful, your Lab has to *like* or at least tolerate being in his crate. Puppies usually acclimate quickly to crates; an adult dog that hasn't had any crating experience may take longer. You may also need to experiment a little with crate types to see whether he likes a den-like experience or a more open, I-can-see-everything kind of crate.

The following are suggestions to help your Lab adjust to his crate.

- **Keep the crate in a busy spot in the home.** Labs like to be involved with their families and in the middle of all the action.
- **Keep the door open.** Allow your Labby free access to his crate, so he can go there to snuggle up any time he wants.
- **Toss treats inside to encourage an adult dog to enter his crate.** Older dogs may be less sure of going into a crate. (A rescue dog may associate the crate with bad things from his former life.) Help him learn that good things happen when he goes in his crate by making the crate a source of treats.
- **Halftime!** If a dog is very resistant to going into a crate, take the top off. Put his bedding in the lower half of the crate and let him get used to the scent and sound of lying down in his crate-bed. Reintroduce the top of the crate later.
- **Put him in his crate with a yummy chew or a safe bone to gnaw on.** Give him something that will occupy him for a little while when he is in his crate. You can feed him in his crate, too. More good things are happening!
- **Encourage napping in the crate.** Keep his bedding in the crate. Make sure it is always clean, dry, soft, and warm.

When the New Lab Is Dog #2

Many dog owners today are *multiple*-pet owners. For the social Labrador, having a play buddy can be a great thing. However, don't assume that just because you are bringing a Labrador Retriever puppy or adult into your home, your resident dog is going to be pleased with the new situation. A recent study noted that the reason *most* dogs were returned to shelters is that they were placed in a home with another dog . . . and the two dogs didn't get along. Your goal should be for the new dog and the resident dog to tolerate each other well. (If they turn out to be inseparable BFFs, you've struck gold.)

First Impressions *Do* Count

The good news is that given time and a little work on the owner's part, *most* dogs (and dogs and puppies) can learn to get along. How long it will take for a new Lab puppy or dog to be smoothly integrated into a dog family hinges on each dog's temperament, the dogs' tolerance levels, how territorial the resident dog is, and how good a leader the owner is.

Helpful Hints

Most dogs tolerate puppies very well and forgive them for transgressions—more than they would an adult dog. However, you'll find that some older dogs get irritated easily by a puppy's constant motion. Respect the older dog's wishes and don't let the pup be too great a pest.

BE PREPARED! Crate Considerations

Crate Type	Pros	Cons
Plastic shell (break down into two pieces)	Easily cleaned, lightweight, approved for airline travel, least expensive, "den-like" for dogs that like to feel enclosed	Less ventilation than wire crates, bulky when stored or carried
Wire crate (can be purchased as collapsible)	Excellent ventilation, allows dog to see everything around him; easier to store or carry when collapsed	Not approved for airline travel, heavy, more expensive, a little more involved to clean with removable tray
Soft-sided carrier	Easily transportable, reasonably priced, approved for in-cabin airline travel	Only for very young puppies for a very short period of time; not suitable for house training; only for carrying from car to veterinarians office or flying
Screen and plastic piping crates	Excellent ventilation, lightweight, medium cost, easily collapsed and stored or transported	Only for supervised crate time (i.e., while in the shade at a dog show or hunt test); dog can easily chew or bull his way out of crate

Perhaps most important is the initial meeting. Lasting impressions (and affronts) can be made within seconds of dogs meeting each other. To prevent any doggie faux-pas from being made, try the following neutral approach.

- **Introduce the dogs on neutral territory.** Take any territorial behavior out of the equation by introducing the dogs in a neutral area, such as a park.
- **Try side-by-side walking.** Enlist a friend or family member to help you walk the dogs on leashes for 10 or 20 minutes. Your goal is to walk the dogs and have them not show any interest in each other *or* have the dogs showing all play, and positive behaviors and body language.
- **Allow the dogs to visit through a dog gate or exercise pen.** This allows both dogs to sniff each other and show appropriate, good behaviors. If you see any hard staring, stiffening of bodies, or fearful body language, separate the dogs from

HOME BASICS
Prepare Your Children

If you have young children, make sure that they know the dog rules. In today's society, we expect much more of our companion dogs. Labs are terrific creatures, *but they shouldn't be expected to be perfect.* To prevent any misunderstandings—a situation in which your Lab feels he must stand up for himself—make sure young children know the basic tenants of dog ownership:

Thou shall not put thy face in the dog's face.

Thou shall not curl up in the dog's crate with or without the dog.

Thou shall not startle the dog while he is sleeping; thou *shall* say the dog's name first before petting him.

Thou shall not poke, pinch, pull, or otherwise tease or hurt the dog; and if the dog has one of thy toys in his mouth, thou shall *always* ask a parent to take the item away from the dog—and then thou shall not leave thy toys lying on the floor.

the gate. Keep initial introductions short and separate before any poor behaviors emerge.

- **Be sure to praise good, positive behaviors.** Both new and resident dog need to be praised for good, positive, friendly behaviors.
- **Make the resident dog feel special.** Give your resident dog more walks, more meals (separate his normal portion into smaller servings so that he can get fed when the new puppy gets fed, too), more toys, and more attention. These things will help to make your current dog feel like all these good things are associated with the arrival of the new puppy or dog.

House Rules

The amazing thing about Labrador Retrievers is that *they never forget anything . . . ever.* That's a great thing when it comes to training your Lab and raising him to be a good companion. It's not a great thing when your Labby gets mixed messages.

CAUTION

Never leave infants, toddlers, or young children alone with a Lab—either a puppy or a rescued adult dog. If you can't supervise, separate.

Specifically, set the rules of the house *with your family* from day one. Everyone needs to know that if they allow the puppy or dog to do

something just once, it could be days, weeks, or months before your Lab is willing to abide by the rules. In other words, if your Lab is not going to be allowed in the recliner when he's an adult, don't bring him up in the chair when he's a puppy.

One of the hardest things for families to stay firm with is feeding the Lab from the table. Puppies are adorable, they have dark eyes that plead, and they look hungry. Don't break down and feed the pup from the table. When you stop giving him table scraps, he'll whine, cry, bark, put his paw on your leg, and generally act very obnoxious. Stand firm and make sure your family members do, too!

Identification Options

Puppies get lost. Adult dogs get lost. If your Lab has identification, you have a much greater chance of recovering him if he gets loose.

Tags

This is the first form of ID that people look for with a lost dog. Make sure your Lab's tags are current and readable. You don't want the finder of your Lab to do a rubbing on the tag to find the engraved contact information—because chances are, it won't happen.

Consider putting your *cell phone* number on your dog's tag. If you're out looking for your lost Labby, you won't be home to take the call if someone finds him. Also, if you're traveling and your Lab gets loose, your *only* chance of finding him while you're still in the area is to have that cell phone number available.

Permanent IDs

If your Lab doesn't have tags and winds up at a rescue or shelter, he will be scanned for a microchip and maybe searched for a tattoo. Tattoes are an excellent form of permanent identification; however, the person who finds your dog has to know where to look *and* possibly shave your Lab's inner thigh to find the tattoo. If you tattoo your Lab, make sure you wait until he is fully grown, so the tattoo doesn't stretch and become unreadable. Also, remember to *register* the tattoo information with a reliable national registry.

Microchips are implanted between the dog's shoulder blades, and though these tiny things (the size of a grain of rice) sometimes travel a little from the implanted location, they rarely fail and can almost always be scanned. Veterinarians, rescues, shelters, and animal control facilities all have scanners (or know where to find one). Once the chip is scanned, the next call will be to locate you. Make sure you keep your contact information up-to-date; always list a cell phone number.

Important First Appointment

Most puppy contracts require that the puppy have a well visit with the veterinarian to confirm that the puppy is in good health. Make sure you schedule this appointment before picking up your puppy. Often contracts require that the appointment be held within 24 to 48 hours of receipt of the puppy. If you pick up your puppy on a Friday and can't get an appointment until Monday, the guarantees in the health contract may expire.

FYI: Labrador Retriever Development

Stage	Abilities
Neonatal (birth to two weeks)	The pup is born with his eyes and ears closed and is barely able to wriggle around
Transitional (two to three weeks)	During this time period, the pup's eyes open, his ears are more fully developed, and he is beginning to get around a little better
Socialization (three to twelve weeks; possibly to thirteen weeks)	The time period during which the puppy's experiences with other dogs and people make the greatest, most lasting impression on the pup
Adolescence (thirteen weeks to six or seven months)	The puppy is still learning a lot during this time and his body is quickly developing. Teething occurs between four and five months of age. House training usually becomes quite reliable by sixteen to eighteen weeks
Maturity (sort of)	Sexual maturity (if the dog is still intact) is achieved between six or seven months and a year. The Lab will have its full height, but will continue to fill out and mature over the next eighteen months to two years. Adult calmness may not occur until four years or more

House-training Made Easy

All Labs can be trained to be reliable in the home. Exceptions would be a dog suffering from one of many possible diseases or conditions, such as urinary tract infection, diabetes (a higher intake of water means more accidents), incontinence, canine cognitive dysfunction, and separation anxiety.

Barring any health issues, training a Labrador to be reliable in the home is relatively easy *if* you follow a few basic rules.

1. **Respect the space.** A young puppy will keep his sleeping and eating area clean and will go to the far end of the whelping box to relieve himself. When he's older, and in your home, he still has the same instinct *not* to dirty his sleeping and eating areas. Therefore, if he is contained in an area that is small enough that he can't relieve himself away from his bedding, he's going to "hold" as long as he can. A comfy crate is usually a good starting point for house training at home. The crate should be just big enough for the puppy or dog to stand up, turn around, and lie down comfortably.
2. **Set reasonable limits.** Young pups can't "hold" that long. Added to that, every little thing makes them want to relieve themselves—hard

puppy play, eating, drinking, any kind of excitement, waking up from a nap . . . all good reasons to have to go *now*. Understand your puppy's age limits for "holding" and don't extend him past his limits.

3. **Increase his space limits** *gradually.* Most accidents happen when a puppy's (or dog's) space is increased too quickly. A reasonable progression would be from a crate to a crate in a small exercise pen, to a crate in a larger exercise pen, and then to a small room with a cleanable floor (such as a kitchen). Allowing a Lab of any age full access to the home may not come for months or even a year.

SHOPPING LIST

House-training Supplies

Some products help to make your job of house-training and cleaning accidents a little easier.

✔ Crate

✔ Exercise pen (also called an X-pen)

✔ Newspapers or pee pads to line the crate or exercise pen

✔ Stain and odor cleaner—these products break down urine into smaller components that do not smell and are not recognizable to the dog as urine

✔ Paper towels

✔ Dog gates—these are useful to block off access to other rooms and contain the Lab in one area (until he's big enough to jump, climb over, or bull his way through. . . .)

BE PREPARED! Sample Young Puppy House-training Schedule

Time	Activity
6:00 A.M.	Relieve, feed, water, exercise
7:00 A.M.	Relieve again, confine*
9:30 A.M.	Relieve, water, confine*
12:00 P.M.	Relieve, feed, water, exercise
1:00 P.M.	Relieve again, confine*
3:30 P.M.	Relieve, water, confine*
6:00 P.M.	Relieve, feed, water, exercise
6:30 P.M.	Play with puppy, watch for signs that he needs to "go," take out as needed, and provide constant access to cool, clean water
10:00 P.M.	Relieve, more exercise (if puppy is "wired" and can't settle down). If the puppy needs to drink, take him out to relieve himself one more time just before you go to bed
10:30 P.M.	To bed!
3:30 A.M.	Relieve. As the puppy gets older, sleeps more soundly, and is better able to hold his urges through the night, this mid-night break will shift to 4 A.M., then 5 A.M., etc., until he's able to sleep through the night
6:00 A.M.	Up and at 'em again!

*Confine to the space that the puppy will keep clean. Initially this will be a crate, but that can increase to a crate or bed in an exercise pen. When you are able to keep your eye on the puppy, he can be in an exercise pen in the room with you or "free" *if you are keeping a close eye on him for "I need to go" body language.* Adult dogs should be confined to crates when the owner is not home, but should be okay (if they've just relieved themselves outside) loose in the same room with the owner. Watch for males that mark, however!

4. **Keep a watchful eye on him when he's loose.** Look for the classic body language of "I need to go": cessation of play, sniffing, circling, and/or moving away from everyone (farther away from his "area"). Carry or move him swiftly outside so he can relieve himself in the correct area.
5. **Praise good behavior.** When you take him outside and he relieves himself, praise him! Good boy! When he has an accident inside, do nothing. If you catch him in the act, you can say "Ah!" or "No!" to stop the flow and quickly whisk him outside. When he finishes outside, praise him, and then go back in and clean the mistake thoroughly. Remember, a dog never has an accident to spite you or to be mean.
6. **Review steps one through five.** If your puppy or adult dog has an accident, see what you might have done wrong in your training. Did you ask the dog to "hold" too long? Did you increase his space too quickly? Figure out where you made *your* mistake and make it easier for your Labby.

Chapter Five

Living with a Lab

The Labrador Retriever is a fun-loving, enthusiastic, willing companion. He is considered possibly one of the friendliest dogs among both people and other canines; however, social Labs don't happen entirely on their own. Behind every people-loving, dog-friendly Labrador, there is an owner who took the time to socialize his or her dog.

Labrador Retriever Behavior

One of the reasons the Lab is such a popular dog among pet owners is that traditionally, the breed *does* have a great temperament and it didn't take too much work to transform a congenial puppy into an outgoing adult. Of course, the expectation for a Lab to raise himself to become the perfect pet is unrealistic—even if the puppy has the genetics for a great temperament.

If a puppy is raised in such a way that he has no experience with people or the experiences he has are bad (i.e., a dog attacks him or a person physically abuses him), even the best-bred, friendliest puppy could grow up to be a fearful, overly sensitive, or reactive adult.

Whether your Labby is born with the genetics for a terrific, even temperament or has the propensity to be a little less than perfect, you *can* raise a wonderful pet *if* you provide your Lab with positive socialization experiences.

Helpful Hints

Practice Helps

Puppies are born with the innate knowledge of basic doggie body language. If a young dog doesn't continue to interact with other dogs in a positive way, his language skills can actually get rusty.

Reading Your Lab's Body Language

Correctly reading your Lab's body language is an integral part of ensuring that every social experience is a positive one. Fortunately, Labs tend to be very expressive.

They have a big, sweeping tail that's easy to read, their faces are very communicative, and with the Lab's big, loose body, it's easy to see when the dog's intentions are good. It's equally as obvious to see when the Lab is frightened by something, or is expressing aggressive behaviors. The trickier part is detecting a Lab's *transition* from a happy dog to a position of flight or fright.

Fun Facts

Smiling Labs

Yes, some Labs do try to imitate the human smile. It looks goofy and is often misinterpreted as baring teeth, but it's a very submissive, friendly gesture and is accompanied with a happy, loose body.

Signs of a Happy Lab

The key here is to look for a big, loose, relaxed body. The dog's tail is wagging *loosely*. His body is relaxed and flexible and has that swinging look to it when he walks and trots. His ears are relaxed, his eyes are calm, and his pant is happy and a result of exercising, not nervousness.

Signs of a Fearful Lab

A cringing body, tucked tail, ears laid back against the neck, half-moon eyes (the eyes move but the head doesn't, so the whites of the eyes are shown), dilated pupils, and nervous panting (usually at a faster rate than exercise-induced panting). The dog may also whimper, cry, or try to retreat or hide behind the owner. Raised hackles can also be a sign of extreme fear (but it can also indicate aggression). If the dog cannot escape, he may shift into aggressive behaviors to give himself more room between himself and the "scary" person or thing.

Signs of Aggression

Body language that indicates a dog is posturing or ready to fight may include any combination of the following: a stiff, taut body; the appearance of standing on his toes; straining forward; hackles up on the back; ears tersely forward; a stiff, raised tail (the tail may be wagging but the wag will be rigid); hard eyes or intense staring; and/or the cessation of panting. Overall, the look is one of hardness, stiffness, and a dog that is ready to blow. The dog may then progress to growling, snarling, snapping, and lunging.

Recognizing the Transition

The key to successful socialization—whether socializing your dog with people or other dogs—is to recognize when the puppy or dog is in a happy state and to recognize *the transition* out of a happy state.

Most dogs, if you're watching carefully, will move into a state of transition in which the dog isn't showing happy body signs but hasn't moved into fear or aggressive behaviors. *This is your cue! This is the moment that you need to recognize and act upon.* If you are looking for and can recognize this moment, you can control the situation and keep all of your Lab's experiences positive!

Backing Out Gracefully

So, what exactly do you do when you see your Lab shift into uncertainty? It depends on the situation.

If your Lab is off leash, allow him to move himself to a more comfortable distance from the person. Do not allow the person to reach out toward your dog. Instead, ask the person to allow your Lab to make his own approach. This usually takes just a second or two, though a timid dog may take slightly longer to warm up.

If your Lab is on leash, call him to you *or* step between your dog and the approaching person, moving your dog away from the individual. You'll want to move your Lab to a location where he is again showing happy body language. Often, when the

PERSONALITY POINTERS
Labrador Retriever Body Language

Lab Mood	Friendly, Relaxed	Transitioning
Head Carriage	Relaxed, easy head position; may dip into a play bow with rear end up and chest lowered to ground	Head may rise or lower slightly depending on whether dog is becoming frightened or feels he needs to defend himself
Eyes	Calm in expression, brows rise and fall inquisitively	No longer relaxed but not yet stressed in expression
Ears	Relaxed, may be forward and alert if getting ready to play or concentrating	May be alert and forward or shift backwards
Mouth	Either comfortably closed, slightly open and neutral in position; or panting and wide open	Mouth closes if he has been panting; or, may begin panting if previously mouth was closed
Body	Loose bodied and without tension; weight is balanced on all four legs; or, if in a play bow, the body may be wriggly and a little coiled appearing	Body begins to lose its looseness
Tail	Relaxed tail position; loose, big wagging tail; speed may increase with happy excitement; may wag in a big circle	Wagging stops or is uncertain and smaller in range; possibly stiffer or tail drops
Voice	Labby is quiet or if he's greeting or seeking attention, he may elicit big happy barks	Dog goes silent; the silent dog may woof, whine or growl softly; or, pitch of voice may raise or lower

Stressed	Fearful	Aggressive
Neck may stiffen, or head may lower	Head slightly lowered, giving the appearance of looking upward	Neck stiff, head may be pulled back slightly or may lower in a threatening position
Pupils dilated; blinking; tightening of lids; aversion to eye contact	Pupils dilated; half-moon eye; tightening of lids; aversion to eye contact	Pupils dilated; narrowing or tightness around eyes; threatening, direct stare
Ears shifted backward or forward and alert; or spread sideways	Pulled back flat against neck	Ears extremely forward and tense
Panting not exercise induced; lip-licking; yawning when not tired	Nervous panting with lips drawn back	Tightly closed mouth; lips may be pulled back or pursed forward; may progress to snapping
Body begins to tense; may transition back and forth from loose body to tense body	Tense; possibly trembling; may run or give the appearance of wanting to run away; legs crouched; piloerection (coat may raise erectly from neck to tail); may urinate submissively or attempt a submissive greeting; may flop onto back exposing belly	Body gives the appearance of being extremely taut and "big"; may appear to be standing on the tips of the toes; piloerection (coat may raise along back from neck to base of tail)
No tail wagging, uncertain wagging or increased rate of wagging with nervous excitement; may make multiple transitions from happy to fear to aggressive tail positions	Very low or tucked tail; may or may not be wagging	Very high tail carriage that is erect at the base of the tail; no wagging or more often the tail wags very stiffly
May be silent or could be whimpering, whining, crying; may also growl, snarl or bark	No sound or may be high-pitched whimpering, crying, or barking	No sound or low growling; low pitched snarling; barking; snapping or lunging

FYI: Subtle Signs of Stress

Dogs can experience stress just as people can, except they can't verbalize what is bothering them. If you know your Lab, you will be able to recognize his body language and know when something in his environment is causing him some concern. Signs to watch for include the following:

- Panting—not from heat
- Yawning
- Avoidance of eye contact
- Shaking (for no apparent reason, such as shaking off water)
- Stretching
- Lip licking/smacking
- Scratching (an out-of-place behavior)
- Closed mouth (when previously panting)
- Clawing, jumping (in a semi-panicked way)
- Drooling (not food triggered)

pup or rescued adult is able to observe from a comfortable distance, he can size up the situation on his own terms. Move him closer to the person as he indicates.

Do not pull, push, or move your Labby closer to a person if he's not showing completely happy, loose-bodied behaviors. Unlike a toddler or young child, with whom you can reason and explain why it's okay to say hello to Ms. Smith, a dog will only feel more trapped, the closer you move him toward the scary person.

Socialization Techniques

So, you know that if you're going up to a person to say "hello," you need to be paying attention to your dog. You need to know your dog, recognize when he's transitioning from happy body language, and remove him from situations before he becomes uncomfortable.

But are there ways to socialize and ways not to socialize a dog? There really aren't too many ways to mess up a meet-and-greet (if you keep things *positive*), but following are some ideas to better control the situation and help ensure that greetings go smoothly.

With People

Usually, socializing a Lab puppy with people is very easy. Everyone wants to meet, pat, and hold the Lab puppy, and most Lab puppies are more than happy to be the center of everyone's universe. It's a win-win situation.

Take advantage of this cute stage of the Lab puppy so that when he's bigger and older, his socialization will be simply a continuation of his puppy work.

With the adult Labrador, it is important to continue his socialization skills. Dogs can develop fears or get a little rusty in their appropriate greeting behaviors. If you've adopted an adult Lab, be particularly observant of his body language and any transitions. Make sure you can fully read his intentions before you start introducing him to strangers. Additionally, give him a little time to bond with you—several days to a week—so that when he approaches a potentially unsettling situation, he trusts you and can approach the situation with more confidence. The rule of thumb here is that if the Lab is not straining to meet someone with completely relaxed body language, you should approach the meeting as you would with a fearful Lab (see "Dealing with the Fearful Lab," page 76).

Helpful Hints

Quality vs. Quantity?

Strive to make positive, friendly meetings with as many people as you can; however, ultimately it is far more important that the meetings be of good quality (completely positive) rather than be numerous and not so positive.

When socializing your Lab with people, you'll have two basic scenarios: meetings in the home and outside the home.

In-home Meetings Meet-and-greets in the home are excellent opportunities for pups and adopted dogs to meet new people in the security and

comfort of their own homes. Additionally, since all socialization is done off leash, the slightly timid Lab is allowed to make his own approach and can back off at any time.

Indoor meet-and-greet tips:

CAUTION

Until your puppy has received his second or third round of vaccinations in the puppy series, for his safety, ask visitors coming into your home to remove their shoes and use hand sanitizer before playing with the puppy.

- Keep a cookie jar by the front door. Encourage visitors to take a small cookie to offer the Lab.
- If your Lab pup or adult is very timid, ask guests to avoid reaching over him, making direct eye contact, grabbing for him, putting his or her face in the dog's face, or making any other sudden or swift moves that could frighten him. *Most* puppies and adults won't have issues with these movements, but less confident dogs can be intimidated or feel threatened by these actions.
- Allow the Lab to approach and back away at will from the visitor.
- Have fun! Give the guest a ball to play fetch with the Lab.
- Praise and reward good behaviors.

Out-and-About Meetings Adult dogs can begin meeting people out and about almost immediately. Puppies will be restricted in where they go (and what surfaces their paws touch) by your veterinarian's recommendations. Some veterinarians recommend waiting until the puppy has his second round of puppy vaccinations; other veterinarians prefer waiting until the puppy has completed his third round of vaccinations. And still others okay social greetings in early puppy training classes (where the floors are sanitized beforehand) with as little as one round of puppy vaccinations.

As you can see, there is a considerable difference in what professionals think is a "safe" time for puppies to set paw in public places. In order not to miss out on the important socialization period (eight to twelve weeks), try splitting the difference: Socialize your pup at home until his second round of puppy vaccinations are complete, and afterward take your puppy places where you can limit his exposure to other dogs and the floor until his vaccinations are completed or your veterinarian okays normal exposures.

Basically, until your veterinarian thinks your puppy is completely protected from deadly viruses (and the risk varies from area to area), you'll want to limit the possibility of your puppy being exposed to dogs that are ill or shedding a virus.

You can still take your puppy places such as the local pet store *if* you keep him from becoming exposed to other puppies and dogs. Do this by bringing your own blanket, sanitary hand wipes, and supply of biscuits. Wipe off a shopping cart with the wipes and place the blanket in the cart. Place the puppy in the cart, keeping the leash on him to prevent him from leaping out. Now you can wheel your pup around, show him off, and allow kids and adults to pet him and offer him biscuits.

Other people-plentiful places you can take your puppy include outdoor cafés (provide your pup with a blanket to lie on), outdoor coffee shops, and hardware stores (the big ones often allow pleasant pups to ride in the carts). If you have access to a doggie stroller, you can also harness your Lab puppy in and take him to even more populated areas, such as strip malls (just walking down the sidewalk can attract a crowd; limit the number of people around your puppy so as not to overwhelm him), outdoor shopping malls, and kids' sporting events.

Outdoor Meet-and-Greet Tips The following are some tips to keep your meet-and-greets with friendly strangers positive and growing experiences for your Lab, whether a puppy or an adult.

- Follow your dog's lead when on lead. In other words, watch for that transition point. If you spot that tail drop and the happy behaviors vanish (or he vacillates between happy and fearful or happy and transitional behaviors), give him more space from the greeting person. Allow him to size up the situation, and when *he* wants to make the approach, allow him to approach.
- Screen friendly strangers. Some people come on too strongly for a less confident dog or puppy. Ask people to meet your Lab only if your Lab is enthusiastic about meeting the person *or* you know that the person is a dog-savvy, dog-friendly human.
- If your Lab balks, do not push him toward the person. Immediately move him to his comfort zone—the distance that he feels safe and his friendly body language returns.
- Give people treats to offer to your puppy or adult Lab. This allows the Lab to make the approach to the person rather than the person to the Lab. And, teaching your Lab that good things come from outstretched human hands is a fine lesson to learn.
- Children tend to flock to Labs, which can make a less confident dog or a puppy feel a little trapped or overwhelmed. To maintain a little control, ask children to line up to meet the Lab. Give each child a biscuit to give him. If you have a puppy, ask the child to sit so the puppy can crawl into the child's lap and give the child lots of puppy kisses. This keeps the child from trying to pick up the puppy or grabbing at him when he's scampering around.
- Recognize that there *will* be people whom

CAUTION

Health Alert

Puppies that haven't received all their vaccinations are at risk of disease. Limit their potential for exposure by selecting fully vaccinated, healthy playmates. Absolutely do *not* take a puppy to a dog park!

your Labrador finds unusual or peculiar. Respect this and allow your Lab to figure things out at his own speed, from what he perceives to be a safe distance.

- If your Lab shows any signs of outward aggression toward anyone, seek the help of an experienced trainer or animal behaviorist (see "Resources," page 169, for a listing of organizations) who can properly determine *what* exactly you're observing (it may not be aggression at all) and then determine the best approach for working toward a solution.

With Other Dogs

Labs love to play, and as a breed, they are recognized for big, boisterous greetings and high-speed, no-brakes play. Non-Labs sometimes misread the Lab's good intentions and find his behaviors either offensive or frightening. When socializing your Lab with other dogs, take the introductions slowly, watch for changes in body language (just as you would when socializing him with people), and try to keep the play fun.

Good Dog Play When choosing playmates for your Lab puppy, try to keep play on an even basis by matching up the dogs by size. The rule of thumb is to limit the size difference between playmates to no more than twice the pup's body weight. In other words, if your puppy weighs 20 pounds, try to find a playmate that doesn't weigh more than 40 pounds, if possible. Likewise, if your adult dog weighs 70 pounds, don't let him play with a dog that weighs less than 35 to 40 pounds. This is simply a safety issue; large variances in size can result in accidental injuries.

When the dogs are playing, be sure to keep it safe and prevent squabbles with the following play tips.

COMPATIBILITY Play Dates

Labs enjoy a lot of physical contact, running, neck biting, and body slamming. The breeds listed here have similar play styles:

- Boxers
- Brittany Spaniels
- Chesapeake Bay Retrievers
- German Shorthaired Pointers
- Golden Retrievers
- Springer Spaniels
- Weimaraners

- **Take time-outs.** High-speed play should be broken up every few minutes to allow the dogs time to settle down (and calm down) before resuming play. Experienced, "good" players will do this automatically. If play is kept at an intense level for too long, someone usually gets offended and then a squabble ensues. Make sure to keep things copacetic by creating time-outs if the dogs don't take them naturally.
- **Watch for balanced play.** Is one dog being chased without being able to return chase? That would be considered one-sided; dogs don't enjoy being the "chasee" all the time. Look for body language to see if any one dog is becoming uncomfortable.
- **Keep the play moving.** It's fun to stop and chat with friends, but if you keep walking through the yard or park to keep the dogs moving (and prevent them from stopping in one place), it tends to keep the play moving along, too.
- **Three can be a crowd.** Some dogs enjoy playing with larger groups; others do best with one other dog. Note how comfortable your dog is as the numbers increase and adjust the play accordingly.
- **Don't believe everything others say.** You know your dog. If he's uncomfortable and you think play is about to go over the top, call your dog out of the group. You'll find many people will tell you, "My dog's friendly!" (when he's a known aggressor) or "Let them work it out" (when a dog is about to get hurt). Trust your instincts and *your* dog savvy.

Dealing with the Fearful Lab

If you've purchased a timid puppy, there are many things you can do to help bring the little guy out of his shell. He may never be a super-bold adult dog; however, with practice and continued socialization throughout his life, he can be a much happier dog around people and/or other dogs.

Working with a fearful puppy is a little easier than working with a timid adult for the reason that a puppy will *typically* not go into fear aggression "mode" until he is at least seven months old (beginning to mature physically). Older puppies and adult dogs, however, may lunge, snap, or bite *if* pushed beyond their capacity for handling a fearful situation.

When helping a timid puppy or dog to become more self-confident and less fearful, abide by the Fearful Five tips:

1. **Allow him to make his own approach.** Allowing him to set the pace of the introduction ensures that he is comfortable.
2. **Work with people you know.** Dog-training clubs are great places. People know dog behavior and are really good with helping those who need assistance.
3. **Ask people to ignore the dog.** When making introductions, you want "strangers" to avoid any actions that could appear frightening to the dog, such as making hard eye contact, reaching over the dog to pat it, grabbing for the dog's collar, or making loud sounds or sudden movements.
4. **Be aware of the Lab's comfort zone.** Know what distance your Lab needs to comfortably observe other people, and work slowly to decrease this distance over time.
5. **Take advantage of off-leash meetings.** Invite people into your home, have them sit down and ignore the dog, and have a supply of treats to give the dog every time he touches or licks the person's hand.

CAUTION

Some timid Labs will never bite no matter how terrified they are. It's just not in their genetic makeup. However, fear biting is a natural response that can be anticipated in any dog, of any breed. So don't assume a fearful Lab won't bite. It's always a possibility.

Remember, with a timid dog, it's important to control meetings so that every greeting is a positive one. It's the quality of the experiences, not the quantity, when it comes to helping a fearful dog become more self-assured.

10 **Questions** on Lab Behavior

1 **My Lab is hyper. Is this normal?** It is not normal for a Labrador to be hyper (high energy coupled with a lack of focus); however, it is normal for young dogs to have extremely high energy levels. To diffuse this excess energy, make sure your Lab receives sufficient exercise. At a minimum, two to three 30-minute power walks, jogs, or bicycling outings per day should help. Also, make sure he's controllable at all times with solid responses for the *sit, down, walk nicely,* and *stay* commands.

2 **How can I get my puppy to stop biting?** Labs are very oral and tend to put everything in their mouths. This includes human fingers, toes, arms, and legs. To control this natural instinct, give your puppy appropriate items to carry and chew on, such as Kongs, Nylabones, and other sturdy toys. Additionally, make sure your pup is well exercised and knows a good *sit* or *down* that can be used to help settle him when he's getting too keyed up playing. Also, if you have children, make sure they are gentle with the puppy and that the puppy also obeys the children's commands for *sit.*

3 **My one-year-old Lab plays so hard! Will he hurt the other dogs at the park?** Labs are naturally physical when they play. As long as your young Lab's playmates are roughly the same size and weight, no one should get injured. Do watch for signs of stress among the other dogs, and remove your dog from play every few minutes to keep him from going over-the-top with his play and offending another dog.

4 **Why is my Lab digging holes in the backyard?** If a Lab is not given enough exercise, mental stimulation, or attention, he will attempt to amuse himself. Your Lab has found hole digging to be entertaining and a way to burn off a little energy. To stop this behavior, increase his exercise, involve him in training (he may really enjoy agility), provide stimulating chew items, and get him out of that backyard and into your home.

5 **How do I get my puppy to stop jumping up on everyone?** Jumping up is actually a friendly, happy greeting. To curb jumping up without squashing a young Lab's enthusiasm for meeting people, teach him a *sit-stay*. When he discovers that children and adults will give him attention and possibly treats, you will find that he will actually *sit* to receive attention without you ever giving him the command. Good boy!

6 **Why is my Lab trying to attack other dogs when we're on a walk?** Leash aggression is very common among Labs and is not indicative of a dog-aggressive Lab. In fact, less secure dogs will often sound awful when on leash and yet will be perfectly mannered or even submissive when meeting and greeting dogs off leash. To help your Labby behave in a more civilized manner when on leash, try the following techniques. 1) Move him farther away from the other dog. Your Labby has a comfort circle, a distance at which he's comfortable observing and doesn't feel the need to create more distance between himself and the other dog. Reward him only when he's silent. 2) Put him in a *down-stay*; it's difficult for a dog to bark in this position. Reward him when he's silent. 3) Keep slack in the leash; a tight leash will telegraph your nervousness directly to him. 4) Distract him with a series of quick obedience commands; reward his good behavior. 5) Slowly work to decrease the distance at which you have to pass other dogs. 6) Keep taking him out on walks.

7 How do I keep my Lab from bolting out the front door? Are you exercising him enough? It's not unreasonable for some Labs to need one or more hours of exercise a day. If lack of exercise is not the issue, teach your Lab a *sit-stay*. When he's solid on this command, practice the *sit-stay* on leash at the front door.

8 How do I stop my Lab from counter surfing? The art of stealing a cooling roast off the kitchen counter while the owner is out of the kitchen for a second is pure Lab. There are a few ways to handle this, but the best solution is simply not to leave food and the dog alone in a room together, unattended.

9 My Lab barks, howls, and urinates every time I leave the house, even if it's just for a few minutes. What can I do? If a dog is extremely anxious and destructive and urinates or defecates within 30 minutes of your leaving your home, he may be suffering from separation anxiety. If your Lab has separation anxiety, there is hope. A good trainer or behaviorist can help you with a desensitization program (these usually take about six weeks), and your veterinarian may be able to prescribe medication specifically for separation anxiety.

10 Why does my Lab growl when he's got his stuffed frog? Will he bite me? Resource guarding is a common behavior among dogs; however, it is undesirable and can become dangerous if the growling escalates to snapping or biting. First, if the behavior occurs only when your Lab is carrying around his stuffed frog, throw Froggy away. If it occurs with more than one item, you'll want to consult a trainer or behaviorist for assistance in reducing this behavior. In the meantime, practice offering a particularly yummy treat as a swap for any coveted item. When your Lab drops the item in exchange for the treat, say "Out!" and reward him with the treat. (Then put away the coveted item.) Practice the *out* command with items that your Labby doesn't guard, so that when he does have something in the future that he doesn't want to give up, and if you don't have a good treat to offer him in exchange, you can use the *out* command. Also, be sure that you work with this Lab every day in obedience exercises and that he gets treats, pats, attention, and other valuable "resources" only if he performs a command for you.

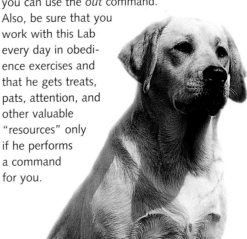

Chapter Six

Health and Nutrition

T he Labrador Retriever is a relatively healthy, sturdy breed—particularly in light of how popular he is. With good preventive veterinary care, proper nutrition, and an owner who keeps a close eye on his or her dog throughout his life for developing conditions, the life of a Labrador can extend well into his senior years.

Preventive Health Care

One of the keys to keeping a Labby healthy is to prevent illnesses from ever having an opportunity to take a toehold in your dog. This preventive care includes vaccinations against deadly diseases, annual physical exams, testing for the presence of worms, and making sure fleas and ticks are held at bay.

Puppy Vaccines

One of the most confusing things about the puppy vaccination series is how the whole thing works. Puppies receive doses of several different vaccinations, several times, over a period of eight to ten weeks. The reason for the series of vaccinations (rather than just one vaccination and they're finished) is a little more complicated.

When the pups are born, they are naturally protected against many diseases because they are ingesting their mother's milk, which is chock-full of antibodies. This immunity does not last forever. The problem is that *no one knows exactly when the puppies lose their immunity*. It could be at eight weeks, ten weeks, or seven weeks and three days. It could be different for each puppy in a litter.

And here's the real problem with "not knowing": Until a puppy loses his natural immunity to disease (i.e., the mother's antibodies are no longer effective), he cannot produce his own antibodies. So, the reason why a puppy is given the same vaccinations several times is to try to time it so that as soon as he becomes susceptible to disease, he receives a vaccination to produce his own antibodies.

BE PREPARED! Choosing a Veterinarian

Do you want a veterinarian who practices with a clinic or has access to the advanced diagnostics and surgical facilities of an animal hospital? Do you prefer working with a veterinarian who has a solo practice or who works with multiple veterinarians? What are your feelings about traditional veterinary medicine, holistic, or a mix of the two? These are choices you'll need to consider when selecting a veterinarian. Perhaps most important—next to your confidence in the veterinarian's level of care and expertise—is that *you* feel comfortable discussing all aspects of your Labby's health with your veterinarian.

When a puppy receives a vaccine, his body creates antibodies when it is exposed to disease. Vaccines are made with viral or bacterial agents in a form that won't infect the dog with the actual disease itself. The dog's body produces antibodies to the specific diseases in response to the vaccine. Even with a series of vaccinations, the puppy is going to be susceptible to disease anywhere from a few days to a couple of weeks. For this reason, many veterinarians are very cautious about allowing puppies to set paw in areas in which there is a high risk of exposure to sick dogs.

Adverse Vaccine Reactions

The Labrador Retriever *is* a breed that has a higher incidence of experiencing reactions to vaccinations. An "adverse vaccine reaction" may range from a minor reaction (slight fever and a little tiredness that generally resolves itself) to a moderate reaction in which the dog becomes itchy, and swelling is apparent around the mouth and eyes, a condition called *urticaria*. This swelling *can* progress to *serious* reaction: anaphylaxis, in which the throat swells shut; seizures; rapid drop in blood pressure; cardiac arrest; and death.

Any reaction to a vaccine is potentially life-threatening and should receive immediate veterinary attention. Once a dog has had a reaction to a vaccine, your veterinarian will either eliminate the vaccine from the dog's care plan (if it's a non-core vaccine), or make sure the Lab has received enough antihistamine before vaccination to prevent a severe response.

The vaccines most likely to cause reactions include rabies, and a noncore vaccine for leptospirosis. The parvovirus vaccine used to be a source of adverse reactions; however, a new generation of this vaccine has less frequent reactions and is considered much safer.

Helpful Hints

The 2006 American Animal Hospital Association (AAHA) Canine Vaccination Guidelines may be viewed as a pdf file at *www.aahanet.org/PublicDocument.*

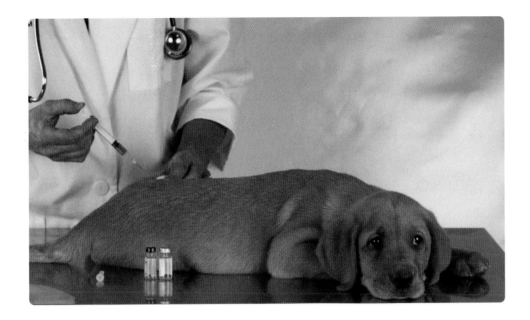

Internal Parasites

It is likely that at some point in your Lab's life (particularly if you enjoy the great outdoors with your pet), he will come in contact with one or more types of worms and/or protozoa. The four most common worms found in dogs are: tapeworms, hookworms, whipworms, and roundworms; the most common protozoa affecting Labs is likely to be giardia, which is ingested through contaminated drinking water (i.e., lakes, streams, ponds, etc.). Many types of preventative heartworm medications protect against hookworms, whipworms, and roundworms.

Intestinal Worms

Worms are spread easily from dog to dog through eggs that are shed in infected dogs' feces. (Tapeworms can take hold if a dog ingests a flea that ate a tapeworm egg. Talk about a small world!) The adult worms survive by either eating partially digested food (the meal of choice for roundworms and tapeworms) or acting like little vampires and sucking blood from the walls of the dog's intestines (how hookworms and whipworms like to spend their free time). Roundworms and hookworms are often passed from the mom to her puppies.

An infestation of worms may cause a change in appetite, weight loss, coughing, diarrhea (with or without blood), a coat that feels rough and dry to the touch, or an overall "look" of not feeling well (i.e., you can't put your finger on it, but you know something is amiss). Then again, a Lab that is healthy and in excellent condition may not show any signs of illness and have a fairly substantial infestation.

FYI: Core Vaccines Timetable

Vaccination	Six Weeks*	Ten Weeks*	Fourteen Weeks*
Canine Parvovirus	X	X	X
Canine Distemper	X	X	X
Canine Adenovirus-2	X	X	X
Parainfluenza Virus	X	X	X
Bordetella	X	X	
Rabies			X
Coronavirus	This vaccination is no longer recommended		

*The series may also be given at eight weeks of age, and regardless of start age, it can be given at three-or four-week intervals.
**High-risk dogs are those that come in contact with large numbers of dogs on a regular basis, such as those that are boarded at a kennel, or compete in performance events or dog shows.

As you can see from the above, detecting the presence of worms just from looking at a dog can be difficult at best. Tapeworms can sometimes be detected by examining a puppy or dog's stool (you may see something that looks like a grain of rice or a short length of worm). Other worms will require a more careful exam of a stool sample by your veterinarian (under the microscope).

The appropriate treatment depends on the type of worms that are found. Usually, your dog will receive a medication for a few days and then will be required to come back for a follow-up fecal exam to make sure the worms are gone. It will also be important to keep your yard as free of feces as possible to prevent reinfection. Regular pickup is important.

Heartworm

Heartworm is a different kind of worm in that it affects the dog's blood vessels and heart, not his intestines. The mode of transmission for heartworm is different, too; infected mosquitoes are the culprits here. For a mosquito to infect a dog with heartworm, the mosquito must have ingested blood from

Booster	Adult Revaccination
One year after completion of puppy vaccinations	Every three years or longer
One year after completion of puppy vaccinations	Every three years or longer
One year after completion of puppy vaccinations	Every three years or longer
One year after completion of puppy vaccinations	Every three years
One year after completion or up to every six months in high-risk** environments	Annually or up to every six months in high-risk** environments
Revaccination dependent on local laws	Every one to three years, depending on local laws

a *dog infected with heartworm*. It takes two weeks *in the mosquito* for the heartworm's "offspring" (microfilariae) to mature into larvae. At the mosquito's next dog meal, the larvae are injected into the bloodstream. If the dog is not on preventive medication, the larvae develop into heartworms. The test for heartworm is a blood test, not a fecal exam.

Fortunately, a heartworm infestation can be completely prevented by giving your Lab monthly oral preventive heartworm medication. If a Lab is infected with heartworms, early detection and treatment are critical in preventing congestive heart failure and death.

FYI: Noncore Vaccines

Vaccination	
Leptospirosis	Recommended only in *some* areas of the country for pets; may be beneficial to hunting dogs that run a greater risk of being exposed to water (such as lakes, ponds, or streams) or soil containing urine from infected cattle, pigs, horses, dogs, rodents, and wild animals; this vaccine has a high rate of serious side effects
Crotalus Atrox Toxoid (Rattlesnake Vaccine)	Developed for protection against the venom of the western diamondback rattlesnake and possible cross-protection against the eastern diamondback; efficacy still being determined
Borrelia burgdorferi (Lyme) Vaccine	Because of its potential side effects, this vaccine is only recommended in highly endemic areas, such as New England. In other areas, dog owners are advised to use topical tick preventives to prevent the tick bite that spreads this disease
Giardia Vaccine	This vaccine does not prevent infection with giardia; however, it may limit shedding of the protozoa and may be of some benefit to large training kennels
Porphyromonas (Periodontal Disease Vaccine)	Efficacy for this vaccine is still being determined

Heartworm infestation treatment is not without risks, but medications and, as a last resort, surgical interventions, can save a dog's life. Note to owners: It's much easier to give a monthly pill to your dog!

Protozoa

There are several different types of intestinal protozoan parasites that could cause a dog trouble, and all tend to cause explosive, watery stools. Several types of protozoan parasites have to be ingested through the stools of infected animals (or the animal itself). Giardia, however, can be ingested through contaminated drinking water—and that includes all the freshwater streams, ponds, rivers, and

BE PREPARED! Mighty Mites

These microscopic parasites can wreak havoc with a dog. Ear mites cause incessant itching in a dog's ears (imagine hundreds of tiny, crablike parasites skittering around in your ear canal eating "ear matter"); "walking dandruff" mites (cheyletiellosis) cause nasty, itchy scaling dandruff skin. If you notice your Lab is shaking his head and scratching his ears *or* he has scaly skin that "walks," see your veterinarian immediately for treatment.

Another mite, *demodex canis*, is often found in the pores of young puppies and rarely causes a problem; however, if a pup's resistance is lowered through stress, disease, diet, or any number of reasons, the mites can take over. Demodectic mange appears as a thinning of hair around the eyes and mouth and on the front legs. This form of mange often clears up on its own; however, if you suspect mange, definitely get your pup to the veterinarian for an examination.

Sarcoptic mange, or scabies, is also caused by a mite. This mite causes extreme itching that often results in horrendous infected sores and hair loss if left untreated. Scabies is also contagious to humans.

lakes where many a Lab hunts or plays. The infection can become very serious very quickly and requires immediate veterinary attention.

Fleas and Ticks

Fleas and ticks are the bane of the dog and dog owner. It doesn't matter where you live, you will have one or the other or both, either seasonally or year-round. Both of these parasites live by feasting on your dog's blood, and both can pass serious diseases or parasites to your dog.

The best way to prevent fleas and ticks from becoming a problem in and out of your home (and on and off your dog) involves a multi-prong approach. Outside the house, keep your grass mowed short. Check your dog for ticks every time he comes inside the house. And, use a prescription, *waterproof* flea and tick preventive on your dog once a month *or* ask your veterinarian about an oral flea preventive (the ultimate waterproof repellent) coupled with a tick collar.

Also, don't forget to treat all areas where your dog sleeps and lies down. Wash your dog's bedding regularly with a sanitary cycle in the washing machine to dispose of any flea eggs waiting to hatch. Vacuum all other surfaces (those you can't throw in the washing machine) thoroughly and seal the bag in a zippered plastic bag before throwing it away.

You may also choose to chemically treat your yard for fleas and ticks; however, this should only be a last resort, as these chemicals can be toxic to your Lab.

Helpful Hints

For additional information on the issues surrounding early altering, consider reading "Long-Term Health Risks and Benefits Associated with Spay/Neuter in Dogs," by Laura J. Sanborn, M.S. (May 14, 2007). This "white paper" includes a bibliography referencing more than 50 scientific research papers reviewed for the paper and can be accessed at the National Animal Interest Alliance web site: *www.naiaonline.org*.

Spay/Neuter

For many years, veterinarians recommended altering pets (spaying females, neutering males) when they were six months of age. Then a recommendation came out for "early" spay/neutering or pediatric altering, which could be performed when the pups were as young as six to eight weeks of age. The main reasons (and they are good ones) for altering pets are to prevent unwanted pregnancies, to prevent some kinds of cancer, and to lessen aggressive behaviors in male dogs.

There are medical benefits to altering pets, and it is certainly easier to manage an altered Lab in a multi-dog home. However, *early* spay/neuters have been linked to an increased risk of two types of cancers common to Labradors, and to urinary incontinence (females), as well as possible increased risks of age-related cognitive impairment, hip dysplasia, and hypothyroidism.

For this reason, it is important to be current on the latest research that is emerging *as it applies to the Labrador Retriever* when weighing the health benefits and disadvantages of when to alter your Labby. For a more informed decision about when to alter your pet, consult with your veterinarian.

Skin Problems

Fifteen percent of all dogs are thought to suffer from atopic dermatitis—itchy, inflamed skin caused by allergies; however, Labs are overrepresented, and run a higher risk. Atopic dermatitis has been shown to have a possible hereditary component. Most of the skin problems that occur in the Labrador are caused by allergies. The allergy could be induced by a single flea bite; airborne allergens such as pollen and molds; atopic allergies from contact with any number of substances (i.e., weeds, plastic bowls, human dander, etc); and food allergies.

When a dog has allergies, he itches. In an attempt to get rid of the itching, he scratches, licks, rubs, and chews. You'll often see him gnawing on his knuckles and paws, scratching his ears, rubbing his face on the floor, or biting and scratching at various other parts of his body. When he nicks the skin—with either a tooth or a toenail—the small cut can become infected. Then you have more chewing, more scratching, more gnawing, and a much bigger problem.

Regardless of what allergy is causing the Lab's skin problems, it is important to not only get the symptoms under control (so he's more comfortable!) but also to find the source of the problem. Your veterinarian may recommend that you see a specialist, a veterinary dermatologist, to pinpoint the source of the allergies and develop an effective treatment plan. A veterinary dermatologist specializes in the diagnosis and management of allergic skin diseases. To find a specialist in your area, you can search online at the Web site of the American College of Veterinary Dermatology (ACVD) under "Find Dermatologist" at *www.acvd.org*.

CAUTION

Hot spots, known to veterinarians as pyotraumatic dermatitis, are open, oozing sores caused by scratching, licking, and chewing. It's most often caused by allergies, but it can also occur in hot, humid climates and/or when a Labby isn't groomed and has a lot of dead undercoat trapped against his skin.

Labrador Retriever Disorders

The Labrador Retriever is at risk for many different diseases. In fact, depending on the source, anywhere from 30 to 50 different diseases and conditions have been seen in this breed.

Before you panic, you should know that many of the diseases on these lists are relatively rare in the dog population. The fact that a particular disease shows up within the Labrador doesn't necessarily make that disease statistically a *huge* problem in the breed or cause for alarm. Certainly, if you own the one dog in 50,000 that suffers from a rare, debilitating disease, it affects *you*.

Most Labrador owners, however, really only need to be aware of the most common diseases and conditions affecting the general Lab population—and to be vigilant in observing any subtle changes in their pets that might indicate a change in the dog's health (see "Detecting Illness, Pain," page 96).

Orthopedic

Joint problems are probably the top health concern among Labrador Retriever breeders, competitors, hunters, and pet owners today. In particular, hip dysplasia and elbow dysplasia are two diseases that, depending on their severity and progression, can be crippling to a young dog.

Hip Dysplasia The hip is a ball-and-socket joint: The head of the femur (the ball) fits into a depression in the pelvic bone (the socket). In a perfect dog world, the head of the femur would fit snugly in the joint and rotate smoothly. When a puppy or dog has canine hip dysplaysia (CHD), the femur is loose in the joint. This looseness causes the femur to bang up against the pelvic bone and cause fractures in both the ball and socket. The fractures heal and leave bony deposits. This creates a worse fit, rougher movement in the joint, more fractures, more deposits, and in turn, an increasingly worse fit.

Hip dysplasia has no cure and is expensive to treat. Nonsteroidal anti-inflammatory drugs (NSAIDs), joint supplements (such as glucosamine and chondroitin sulfate), acupuncture, chiropractic treatment, and vitamin C (an anti-inflammatory) may provide temporary relief and may slow—but do not stop—the progression of the disease. Likewise, proper weight maintenance (every extra pound puts four pounds of pressure on a joint) and exercise (strong muscles help to keep loose joints from moving too much) are important in slowing joint damage but won't stop the destruction of the joint.

CAUTION

Labs tend to be very stoic when it comes to pain. By the time a Lab shows even a small limp or a little tenderness, it may be a symptom of a much bigger problem.

Two types of surgery are available for larger breeds that *do* provide permanent relief: triple pelvic osteotomy (the pelvic bone is cut into three pieces and the entire hip is rotated) and a total hip replacement (virtually the same operation as humans undergo). Though both surgeries have high success rates, they are expensive, and the recovery time (and owner involvement) is four to six weeks.

The importance of purchasing a puppy from a reputable breeder who tests his or her dogs for hip dysplasia (among other hereditary diseases) cannot be stressed enough. If you've purchased a pup with the disease, or adopted an adult dog suffering from CHD, don't put off finding out what you can do to help slow its progression! The sooner you begin treating the disease (and slowing the progression), the more comfortable your Labby will be.

Elbow Dysplasia Similar to hip dysplasia, elbow dysplasia is also a degenerative disease of a joint, and it, too, has a hereditary factor. However, the term *elbow dysplasia* actually includes three different abnormalities: ununited anconeal process (UAP), osteochondrosis (OCD), and fragmented medial coronoid process (FCP). A Labby diagnosed with elbow dysplasia may have one or more of these conditions.

FYI: Other Hereditary Disorders and Diseases

The Labrador is susceptible to several other conditions that have a hereditary basis, including the following:

Dwarfism*: The Lab appears generally normal except that his legs are slightly bowed and abnormally short. This condition is linked with an eye abnormality, called *focal retinal dysplasia*. Surgery may be required to provide relief if the dog suffers from pain in the forelegs.

Exercise-induced Collapse (EIC)**: Usually seen during high-intensity exercise, training, or conditioning of Labs, EIC has no known cure, but many dogs with the condition do fine as pets or even as performance dogs in less stressful sports such as obedience, agility, and even flyball.

Epilepsy: This disease can have many different causes; however, if seizures appear before a dog is five years of age, the condition is generally considered hereditary. Seizures can range from relatively mild and intermittent to severe and regularly occurring. Medical treatments can help limit the frequency and severity of the seizures.

Hereditary Myopathy**: Also known as Labrador Retriever myopathy, this is a rare disease that causes muscle weakness because of a deficiency of a certain type of muscle fiber. Dogs may have mild muscle weakness (and a good prognosis as a pet) or may become very debilitated.

Hypothyroidism**: The thyroid does not produce enough hormones, causing a change in metabolism (weight gain), hair loss, and skin problems. The treatment for the disease usually involves a synthetic thyroid medication that is relatively inexpensive and is given orally.

If any of these illnesses are diagnosed in your Lab, it is important to report it to your breeder. If a pup has a hereditary disease, it means that, depending on the mode of inheritance, one or more of the breeder's dogs are carriers of the disease.

*Carriers of dwarfism can be determined with an eye exam, since the eye condition is linked with the dwarfism gene.
**Genetic tests are available for these diseases.

Elbow dysplasia is treated with arthroscopic surgery, a minimally invasive procedure during which the surgeon goes in and cleans out the joint. Dogs are often using the limb the same day as surgery, and the recovery time is much less involved than surgery for hip dysplasia. Though still expensive, this surgery has a good success rate in relieving the dog of pain and discomfort.

Arthritis Virtually every older Lab will eventually suffer from arthritis in his joints. Labs that are extremely active or that have had an injury to a joint may develop arthritis sooner than the Lab that spends his days participating in nonimpact sports, such as swimming.

Cartilage simply wears away with use and over time, even when a joint doesn't have any abnormalities. When a joint doesn't have much cushioning, it becomes inflamed, which is very uncomfortable, too. The pain of

arthritis can be eased using many different approaches. (For more information, see "Easing Arthritis," page 153.)

Eyes

Labrador Retrievers can suffer from several different eye diseases, such as progressive retinal atrophy (PRA), cataracts, and retinal dysplasia. These diseases cause limited vision or blindness over time. Many eye diseases are believed to have a hereditary basis; therefore, it is important to purchase puppies from breeders who "CERF" their dogs annually (see "Health Screening and Tests," page 42).

The bad news is that many hereditary eye diseases have no treatment, no cure, and no way to slow their progression. The one exception to this is a cataract. Surgery is possible to remove the diseased, clouded lens and replace it with an artificial lens—yup, just like with humans. This surgery does not come without cost or risks; however, if a Lab is affected with cataracts in both eyes, surgery can greatly improve his quality of life if vision is restored to one eye.

With other eye diseases (that aren't operable), the good news is that most (but not all) of them are usually painless and if the disorder is present in only one eye, the dog often adjusts quite

Helpful Hints

A terrific online resource for owners of blind Labs is the Owners of Blind Dogs Web site (*www.blinddogs.com*). This online organization is the site for the Blind Dog e-mail list and the Blind Dog Message Board.

93

well. If the blindness or limited vision occurs in both eyes, the situation is still quite workable, if you are willing to help your dog live comfortably at home and walk him on a leash when he's outside.

Heart

The Labrador Retriever is susceptible to several different heart diseases; however, the heart condition that seems to be showing up with increasing frequency is tricuspid valve dysplasia (TVD). This condition, in which one of the heart valves does not shut tightly and allows blood to leak back through it, is hereditary. Puppies with a slight "leak" may be able to lead normal lives, whereas pups with a severe leak often die before they are a year old.

Symptoms of heart failure include the appearance of "getting fat," which is actually the accumulation of fluid in the dog's abdominal region, and/or the dog being less energetic than before or easily fatigued. Currently, there is no cure or treatment for the condition; however, medical intervention can slow the progression of congestive heart failure and make a dog more comfortable.

Studies are being done to identify the gene that causes this disease in hopes of developing a genetic test that would find carriers.

Gastrointestinal Tract

Of the different disorders that can affect a dog's gastrointestinal system, the most common and most lethal is bloat, or gastric dilatation-volvulus (GDV). With bloat, the dog's stomach becomes distended with gas (gastric dilation) and then *twists*, cutting off blood circulation from the stomach to the dog's intestines, and in turn, to the dog's heart. Though many theories have been researched to try to determine what risk factors increase a dog's chances of suffering from bloat, the only risks linked (so far) with GDV are fearful or excitable behavior, and rapid eating.

Bloat tends to come on very quickly, and in a severe case a dog will be dead within 30 minutes. So, if you suspect your dog may have bloat, *take him to the veterinarian's office immediately and call them on the way to tell them you're coming.* Do not hesitate or wait to see if your dog "gets better."

Symptoms:

- A distended abdomen
- Trying to vomit or belch with no results; nauseated
- Restless
- Shortness of breath
- Appearing "depressed"
- Showing signs of pain

Breed Truths

A recent study looked at a possible connection between adverse weather (a meteorological influence) and the onset of bloat. More research is needed; however, a dog's sensing of adverse weather may encourage GDV risk factors, such as a change in activity levels in dogs, fearful or excitable behavior, and/or rapid eating.

If the stomach has not twisted, the gastric dilation may be able to be treated without surgery. If the stomach has already twisted, surgery is required to save the dog's life. Most Labbies will never have a problem with bloat. If you are one of the ones whose dog *does* bloat, it pays to know the symptoms in advance and the urgency of the situation.

Cancers

Cancer is a growing concern among Labrador Retriever owners and breeders. Statistically, the Lab has a higher incidence of certain cancers, and these cancers are striking at an early age (before the age of eight). The concern among breeders and researchers is that the cancers may have hereditary components.

Currently, the Labrador Retriever is involved in several research projects in search of DNA markers (abnormalities) for hemangiosarcoma (a highly invasive, blood-fed tumor), mast cell tumors (tumors that release chemicals that cause gastric ulcers, internal bleeding, and a range of allergic responses); and melanomas (a cancer of the pigment-producing cells of the skin). The Labrador has also been shown to suffer from osteosarcoma (bone cancer) at an elevated rate, and is also more at risk of suffering from lymphoma (a blood cancer).

With current genetic-based research, it may be possible in the future to determine if a dog carries a gene for a specific cancer. It is also hoped that this research will help develop cures for cancer, not only in dogs but in humans. (Dogs are an excellent model for many human diseases.)

Breed Truths

Cancer is currently the top reported cause of death in the Orthopedic Foundation for Animals (OFA) ongoing Labrador Retriever health survey.

Until this time, it is important for Lab owners to be acutely aware of their dogs' general health, feel daily for lumps and bumps, and seek veterinary advice if any physical or behavioral changes are detected. (See below.) Early detection of many types of cancer greatly improves a dog's long-term prognosis, as well as quality of life.

Lipomas

As a Labrador Retriever ages, you may notice marble-sized tumors that appear just under the skin and seem "loose" or not attached to anything in particular. These are often fatty cell tumors, and though unpleasant to look at, they are mostly benign and are only a cosmetic issue. They may grow quite large, but unless the tumors are in a place that causes your Lab pain (i.e., in the armpit or on the sternum where the dog lies down), they are left in place.

Diagnosis is usually done by aspirating (inserting a needle into the tumor and removing a few cells) the lipoma and examining the cells under a microscope. Lipomas are very common among aging Labrador Retrievers; however, it is wise to have every new lipoma checked by your veterinarian, rather than assuming it's not a cancerous tumor.

Detecting Illness, Pain

Labrador Retrievers are often quite stoic when it comes to showing any outward signs of pain. In fact, some dogs can actually have very serious injuries or advanced disease before anyone detects even the slightest hitch in the dog's gait.

Because it can be difficult to detect injuries or disease in the early stages in dogs such as this, the American Animal Hospital Association released a list in November 2007 of six signs of hidden pain:

1. Abnormal chewing habits
2. Drastic weight gain or loss
3. Avoidance of affection or handling
4. Decreased movement and exercise
5. Excessively licking or biting himself
6. Uncharacteristic "accidents" in the home

If your Labrador shows any of the above signs that he may be in distress, see your veterinarian immediately. Additionally, it's important to recognize

the general signs of a dog in pain, which include panting or quick, shallow breathing; whimpering and crying; restlessness, limping, or stiffness; guarding of injured body part; trembling or shaking; and/or refusing to eat or drink. With a more thorough exam, your veterinarian should be able to uncover the source of your dog's pain.

Dog Food Decisions

If you haven't taken a walk down the dog food aisle in a pet store lately, you might be surprised. You'll find high-quality foods for puppies, adults, seniors, large-breed dogs, and overweight dogs, as well as specialty foods for specific breeds. Then there are foods without grains, foods for sensitive stomachs, all-natural foods, and foods with antioxidants, joint supplements, and/or other special ingredients. Oh, and then there's dry foods, semi-moist foods, canned foods, and frozen meals.

The selection is mind-boggling, to say the least.

A good starting point is the food your Lab puppy or adopted adult is already eating.

Helpful Hints

Want to start a "hot" topic in a Labrador online chat room? Ask when you should make the switch from puppy food to adult food. You will hear everything from 18 to 24 months (when a large breed reaches maturity), to a year (similar to many manufacturers' recommendations), to 6 to 9 months of age (to prevent the Lab's bones from overgrowing his muscles). Talk to your breeder for his or her preferences and/or discuss this issue with your veterinarian.

A sudden change in food can cause gastrointestinal distress, which is the *last* thing you want when you've just brought a new dog into your home. Once your Lab has settled in and is comfortable in his new home, you can consider gradually switching him over to a new food.

When you do look for a new food, choose one that is made by a reputable company and that is considered to be of high quality. Somewhere on the food's packaging, it should say that the food meets all the nutritional requirements as established by the Association of American Feed Control Officials (AAFCO) of either "growth or reproduction" (puppy and nursing females) or "adult maintenance." It is preferable that the food not only meets the nutrient profile but also has passed a feeding trial.

Helpful Hints

10-day Rule

To avoid gastrointestinal upset when switching to a new dog food, gradually mix the new food into the old food over a period of ten days.

In previous years, the guidelines were published with the *minimum* nutritional requirements for dogs. In 2008, the AAFCO released new nutritional guidelines that listed *maximum* levels of certain minerals and vitamins that have the potential of being detrimental if occurring in too great concentrations. Maximums are cited for such ingredients as vitamins A, D, and E, as well as minerals calcium, phosphorous, magnesium, and iron, among others.

Feeding the Puppy

Your puppy will most likely be eating a high-quality puppy food when you bring him home. Most brands are excellent sources of nutrition; however, you might find that your breeder prefers a particular manufacturer over another or that he or she wants you to feed a puppy food for large breeds, to ensure that the Lab puppy doesn't grow too quickly.

Probably of greatest importance, however, is not which high-quality food you are feeding your pup, but *how much* you are feeding him. This is a time of rapid growth for the puppy, and though you want him to have the fuel necessary to grow, you certainly don't want to burden his young, developing joints with too much weight.

Most puppies will not overeat if

Breed Needs

Young puppies, 8 to 12 weeks old, will need to be fed three times a day. Older puppies and adults can be fed twice a day.

- there is no competition for their food (i.e., other dogs);
- the food is dry;
- no liquids such as beef broth, or yummy scraps have been added; and
- the food is picked up after the puppy has had an opportunity to eat for 30 minutes.

The next question is, of course, how much do I feed my puppy? The problem is that every puppy's size is a little different, every puppy's metabolism runs at a different rate (some really burn through their food and others are more efficient and need less food), *and* every pet food has different caloric values, so a cup of one food could have as many calories as three-fourths cup of another food.

The best advice when trying to determine how much to feed your pup initially is to provide more dry food than you think he'll need. *Measure the amount you are putting down for him.* Allow him 30 minutes to eat the food, pick up the remaining food, and measure it. Calculate how much food your puppy just ate. Do this for two days' worth of feedings until you've got a good idea about how much to put down at each feeding.

Feeding the Adult

Adult Labs are notoriously good eaters and have more than a tendency to become obese. Obesity among aging Labs is potentially at the epidemic stages. Allowing your Lab to become obese (20 percent overweight) is perhaps the most harmful thing you can do to his health.

If your Lab is beginning to put on weight, modify how much you are feeding him (measure each feeding!). Or, consider switching your Labby to a weight-reduction food, which provides the nutrition (and bulk) of his former food but not the calories. With a diet food, he can eat the same quantity at each feeding that he was used to eating with his former food but not

consume as many calories. Additionally, if you aren't taking your Labby out for daily walks, now would be a good time to start. If your Lab is expending more calories than he's eating, he will lose weight.

A weight-reduction drug for dogs, Slentrol (dirlotapide), was approved by the Federal Drug Administration in January 2007 and is available to help in difficult cases of obesity. The drug reduces a dog's appetite and fat absorption. It isn't without potential side effects, however, including vomiting, loose stools, diarrhea, lethargy, and loss of appetite.

If, however, you can help your Lab reduce his girth to a more slender, youthful shape through exercise, less calorie dense foods, and better meal portions, it's always better to do this without medications.

A Word on Homemade Diets

It used to be that if you told your friends you were making all your Labby's meals in your kitchen with human-grade foods, they might think you were

FYI: Cooking for Your Lab

A good source for multiple homemade diets is *www.BalanceIt.com*. Developed by a veterinary nutritionist, this website allows you to select a protein (i.e., pan-browned ground beef, skinless roasted chicken breast, baked Atlantic salmon, 2 percent cottage cheese, etc.) and a carb (i.e., cooked, long-grain brown rice; cooked oats; cooked, flesh-only sweet potato; cooked enriched spaghetti, etc.). After you've made your selections, you will be presented with a choice of recipes using these ingredients, in addition to vegetables, oils, and other foods (depending on the recipe), and supplements. You can choose to select either the measurements necessary from a combination of human supplements that are available at drugstores or the Balance IT canine supplement available on the Web site.

crazy (or had way too much time on your hands . . .). With the widespread pet food recall in 2007, the idea of being able to control precisely what went into a Lab's diet suddenly became much more attractive to pet owners.

If you are considering making a homemade diet for your dog, there are a few rules that you *must* follow for the diet to be safe and healthy for your Lab.

1. The diet must be written by a veterinary nutritionist. Too many diets are appearing on the Internet and in books that are promoted as homemade "diets" for dogs. Though these recipes could make for a nice treat or snack, they are not nutritionally balanced.

2. Do not make substitutions unless it is *specifically* allowed in the diet. Creating a balanced diet for a dog is much more difficult than it might seem, and every ingredient not only *counts* but balances another ingredient.

CAUTION

Obese dogs are at greater risk for developing diabetes, as well as for suffering torn ligaments and the early onset of arthritis.

3. Measure precisely. Yes, it makes a difference if that tablespoon of bonemeal is rounded or not! And no, don't throw in extra flax-seed oil just because you can. Again, homemade diet recipes are balanced only if they are followed to a T.

4. Don't skimp. A common problem with homemade diets is that they require the addition of vitamins, minerals, and other supplements. The sources for these ingredients can be expensive, and frequently owners begin to "skimp" by not adding all that the recipe requires or simply not adding the supplement at all. This is not only unsafe but can affect your dog's health in a very short period of time.

Chapter Seven

Training and Activities

L abrador Retrievers can be so intuitive at times that it seems as though they almost teach themselves . . . but don't be fooled. They don't. Raising a well-behaved, obedient pet takes some dedicated work from the owner; however, because the Lab is so willing and ready to learn, the training is not so much a chore as a time to have some fun with your Labby.

A Little About Training the Lab . . .

If you've never trained a Labrador Retriever before, you are in for a treat! This is truly one of the most (if not the most) fun dogs to train. What many pet owners don't realize is that they have more than a century's worth of sportsmen to thank.

The Labrador Retriever was bred to be a *close-working*, personal hunting dog—to stay quietly with his handler until asked to go retrieve a shot bird. Contrast this with other types of hunting dogs that were bred to work at a distance from their handlers, searching for birds so far from their handlers that the dogs can't be seen, and traveling so fast that dog owners must follow on horseback to keep their dogs in sight. The importance here is that the close-working hunting dog (the Lab) is bred to look to his handler for commands. When training your Lab, you will find that he does, indeed, look to you for direction, as opposed to breeds that were bred to work at huge distances from their handlers (the Pointer), which tend to show a more independent streak in training.

Additionally, to be a good retriever, the Lab has to be tireless in performing his job. He needs to have energy to retrieve a bird quickly, and he must be happy to retrieve birds *endlessly* throughout the day. For the pet owner, this translates into a dog that is happy doing multiple repetitions of a task. In other words, where another breed may begin to become bored after being asked to *sit* more than four times in a row, the Labrador will sit *endlessly* if you make the exercise fun.

One of the trademarks of the breed (that was even commented on in transcripts dating back to the days of the St. John's dog) is the breed's sunny disposition. This same cheerful, happy temperament has a lot to do with the Lab's success as a hunting dog: He's eager to please and his spirit is not dampened easily. Some people may even say the Lab is a bit hard-headed at times, because he is so resilient to heavy-handed corrections. You'll find that the Lab performs best with positive, reward-based training and that when he thinks training is fun, you won't experience any resistance to training.

And, perhaps most encouraging for the novice trainer, Labrador Retrievers are very forgiving of handler errors. With some breeds, if you make a mistake in training an exercise (i.e., you

Breed Truths

Labs maintain their puppy energy well into their third or fouth year. Good obedience skills are important in controlling adolescent enthusiasm, when the Lab still acts like a "puppy" but is now in an adult-sized body.

accidentally teach your dog a different behavior than the one you wanted) and then you try to correct yourself, the dog immediately becomes confused, you become frustrated, and the process of retraining the dog takes forever. With the Labrador, it's more like, "Oh. So you want me to do it this way now? Okay. Got it."

The Labrador Retriever, thanks to his centuries of breeding as the ultimate retriever, is an enjoyable dog to train. *Everyone*, regardless of his or her training experience, can train a Lab to obey house rules and learn multiple commands.

Breed Needs

Seniors *love* training, too! For the aging Lab, training sessions are a great reason to get off the couch and go outside for some one-on-one attention and much-needed exercise.

Puppies and Adults

So, what's the difference between training a puppy and an adult dog? Not a whole lot except that with a puppy your biggest challenges will be in working with a shorter attention span and a much higher energy level.

Attention Span The Labrador Retriever is renowned for his intense focus. In fact, much of the breed's success is because of the dog's ability to focus on you and what you are trying to tell him to do. Even though this is a breed that doesn't physically mature until he's 18 months or older, the Labrador can be so mature focus-wise that often he is capable of being trained for (and achieving) advanced performance titles as a year-old dog.

With that said, Labradors are individuals. Some dogs have a keener focus than others. Puppies generally have a much shorter attention span than adult dogs, so you have to adjust your training sessions accordingly. Young puppies benefit from short bursts of training (a few minutes at a time) randomly scattered through-out the day. An adult dog (if he's having a good time) may be fine with a 30-minute training session or a one-hour class.

Energy Level Of course, much of whether a Labrador *can* focus on what you're asking him to do depends on how much energy he's got. Lab puppies, by nature, have a lot of energy. When they're awake, they tend to be going 100 mph. Then, you'll look and they're sleeping just as hard as they were playing just a few minutes before. You can't train when they're zoom-ing and you can't train when they're *zzzzzzzzzing*—so when can you train?

With a puppy, the trick is in diffusing just enough of the pup's liveliness that

FYI: Working with the Rescued Lab

The beauty of positive, reward-based training is that you can literally train your dog in any behavior without ever having to physically move him into a position. This is critically important with the adult, rescued Lab who 1) may not completely trust you yet, 2) might have problems with being touched in certain places because of past experiences or residual pain that you aren't aware of, and 3) is way too big to be forced into a position (i.e., you're not going to win that battle . . .).

he's not distracted with gobs of pent-up energy and yet leaving him lots of get-up-and-go for training. The young adult dog also tends to have quite a bit of energy, and it's important to give him an outlet for his exercise needs, too. A well-exercised dog is a less-distracted dog.

Foundations for Teamwork

Entire volumes have been written about training, how dogs learn, and what works and what doesn't. And, virtually every trainer has a different approach to training, different ways to teach the exact, same exercise, different techniques to get a dog to do what you are asking him the first time rather than the second, third, or umpteenth time.

To some degree, every trainer who gets results (no matter how harsh the methods are) is correct in that their training approaches work. But to get the *most* out of your Lab's good nature, enthusiasm, and real desire to please, you simply cannot go wrong with positive, reward-based training. It works beautifully with Labrador Retrievers. Whether you want to go on into performance events or not, you will have established a solid basis from which to build. And, you will have the tools to be able to train your Lab to do virtually *anything*.

How Your Lab Learns

Without bogging you down with a lot of technical jargon, the basis of positive, reward training is twofold. First, the dog is trained to provide a behavior in response to a voice command, hand signal, or other cue. This training is *positive* in that no negative means (punishments, corrections) are used to get the dog to provide the desired behavior.

For example, to teach a dog to *sit*, a treat would be used to lure the dog into position. That's a positive approach. The reward comes in when the dog receives the treat for a successful *sit*. If he doesn't provide the correct behavior, nothing happens. The correct behavior is reinforced with a reward; the incorrect behavior achieves nothing for the dog.

A negative approach would involve wrestling the dog into position and popping him with the choke chain, shocking him with an electric collar, or swatting him on the behind if he breaks the *sit*. Certainly, you can teach a Lab using negative reinforcements. The basis of operant conditioning is that a dog will learn to perform a task either to avoid pain (negative reinforcement) or to achieve a coveted resource, or something of value to the dog, such as food, a toy, praise, or physical pats (positive reinforcement).

However, owners and trainers alike have found that a positive, reward-based training program not only gets fast results (and the dog retains what he has learned just as well as with negative training methods), but that dogs trained using a positive, reward-based training system are happy and eager to please. It changes the dynamics of the dog's training and the relationship between the dog and handler—and it changes it in a good way.

Helpful Hints

Teaching the Clicker

You want your Labby to connect the sound of the clicker with a treat reward. To do this, practice by clicking and treating. Hold the treats in one hand and the clicker in the other. <click>, treat, <click>, treat, <click>, treat. Your Lab will catch on *very* quickly.

How Positive, Reward-based Training Works

Basically, the key to this type of training is *setting your dog up for success*. Since you aren't going to be correcting or punishing your dog for an incorrect behavior, you'll need to make sure that he provides the behavior you want, so you can reinforce this behavior with a reward. In other words, you will need to teach him new skills in a way that he almost can't fail. As he catches on to what you are training him to do, you will make the exercise more difficult in very small increments. Remember, the more times he does something correctly (without errors), the faster he will progress.

Here's a quick version of how the process goes.

The Timing of "Behavior * Command * Mark * Reward * Release"

First and foremost, when teaching a new skill, the *command* is spoken when the Labby is in the correct position (providing the desired behavior). So, for example, if you are teaching the *sit*, you will first position your pup into the sitting position using a treat as a lure, and *the moment his rear is **firmly** planted on the floor* THEN you say "Sit!" If you say "Sit" before you lure your puppy into position, he will not connect the command "Sit" with the actual behavior of sitting—he'll connect "Sit" with halfway sitting.

Helpful Hints

If at any time your Lab seems to move slowly through an exercise, this means he is confused, not sure of himself, or lacks confidence that what he's doing is actually correct. Make the exercise easier immediately for the next few repetitions until you can restore his enthusiastic and decisive responses.

Once in the correct position, you want to "mark" this behavior as correct by saying "Yes!" or "Good!" If you are training using a clicker, you would <click> the moment the Lab sits correctly. Marking a behavior seems a little bit like overkill in the beginning stages of training; however, as you advance and begin teaching your Lab more difficult exercises, the "mark" is critical in giving your Lab a precise point at which he is correct.

Next comes the reward. The reward (which can be a treat, praise, pats, a toy, etc.) follows the mark. After the reward comes the release command (i.e., "Okay!" "All done!"). Then, you repeat the exercise to help solidify what your Lab is learning.

Putting it all together, here's how the entire training sequence goes:

1. BEHAVIOR—Lure the dog into position using a treat as a guide (lure shaping).
2. COMMAND—Say the command *when* the dog is in the correct position.
3. MARK—Pinpoint the correct behavior with a verbal (Yes!) or mechanical signal (a click from a clicker).

4. REWARD—Reward the behavior with your Lab's favorite treat, play with a ball, tug on a towel, etc., followed by the ultimate reward of physical praise (pats and rubs).
5. RELEASE—Allow your Lab to break from his position with a command, such as *Okay!* or a solid pat on the chest.
6. REPEAT—A Lab should complete the exercise eight to ten times correctly *and with confidence*, before the exercise is made any more difficult; however, with a puppy the repetitions should be broken up through the day so as not to lose the pup's focus.

The Basics

Many pet owners find that four basic commands can make a world of difference when it comes to reining in a rambunctious puppy or helping an I-don't-know-any-house-rules rescued adult dog adjust to family life. The Fave Four are *sit, stay, down,* and *come.*

Sit

When can you use the *sit*? This command is helpful in preventing a bouncy Lab from jumping up on visitors. It's also helpful in getting a rowdy puppy to settle down quickly, and in keeping an excited dog from jumping up and knocking his food bowl out of your hands at suppertime. Regularly asking your Lab for a *sit* throughout the day also helps to exercise your leadership in a gentle, nonconfrontational way.

To teach the *sit*, follow these steps.

1. **BEHAVIOR**—Holding your Lab's collar gently (this is just so wriggly puppies don't go running off), take a treat in the other hand and slowly pass it from your Lab's nose to the back of his head, between his ears. Keep the treat in a closed hand and pass it so closely to the dog's head that you almost touch him. What will happen is that he will rock back to follow the treat and *sit*.

2. **COMMAND**—When his rear end is *firmly* on the ground (not dancing, not almost there, not up and down), say "Sit!"

3. **MARK**—Say "Yes!" or <click>.

4. **REWARD**—Give your Labby the treat you used as a lure. What a good boy!

5. **RELEASE**—Say "Okay!" and/or give a pat on the chest and some playtime.

6. REPEAT—After eight to ten repetitions (these can be spread out for puppies), your Lab will start to show you that he understands what you're asking him to do. He will follow the treat easily and move into the *sit* position quickly.

At this point (and not before) you can begin "backing up" the command. So, with the *sit*, you'll give the command when he is *almost* in position. When he completely sits, *then* you'll MARK the correct position verbally or with a click. REWARD, RELEASE, REPEAT until he's getting it correctly *and with confidence* for eight to ten repetitions.

Continue to back up the COMMAND ("Sit") to the point where he is beginning to fold himself into a sit. When you have success with that, you can give the command when you just begin to pass the treat over his head, then when you have the treat in front of his head. Finally, you'll be able to back it up to the point where you don't have to lure him into a *sit* at all. Yay! He knows his *sit*!

Stay

The *stay* command can come in handy for many different situations. At the front door, a *sit-stay* can be used to prevent a dog from bolting. At the top of the steps, a *sit* or *down-stay* can be used to prevent your Labby from dragging you faster down the steps than you want when you start out on your morning walk. A *down-stay* is handy for keeping your Lab quiet while you are eating your dinner.

The *stay*, of course, can be taught with any position—the *sit*, *down*, or even a standing position. Since you've just taught your Labby the *sit*, we'll use the *sit-stay* as an example for how this command is taught.

FYI: Head Halters

If you've adopted a heavy-pulling adult Lab, consider using a head halter. Several companies make these training tools. It is made of a loop that goes over the dog's muzzle (he can open his mouth) and behind his ears. The leash clips to a point under the dog's chin. When the dog pulls, he hits the end of the leash, forcing his head to turn back toward you—and his body follows. So now he's facing you rather than pulling forward. Oops. Not what *he* wanted to do.

Typically, it takes only a walk or two with this device on for the Lab to learn how the system works and to have him walking comfortably alongside you.

1. Snap a leash onto your Lab's collar.
2. Stand by his right side (dog on your left).
3. Give him the *sit* command.
4. Put your left hand, fingers down (and palm facing your Lab) directly in front of your Lab's nose. While moving your hand in a short, right-to-left motion, say "Stay."
5 Wait a second or two, and then MARK—REWARD—RELEASE—REPEAT. (Remember, "repeat" for eight to ten solid repetitions before making the exercise more difficult.)
6. Make the exercise more difficult by adding a little distance to the *stay*. Repeat steps one through four and then take one step to the right and step immediately back to the dog. MARK—REWARD—RELEASE—REPEAT.
7. Add time to the stay by stepping to the right, staying in this position for several seconds, and then stepping back to the dog. MARK—REWARD—RELEASE—REPEAT.
8. Continue to add either more distance or more time (but not both!) to the exercise until you can walk to the end of the leash, stand there for a minute, walk back, walk around your dog, and return to his side.

Down

The *down* can be used to settle an excited Labby and to silence a barking dog (the *down* position makes it physically difficult for a dog to bark). The *down* is also a submissive position, so asking your dog to *down* several times a day helps to strengthen your role as his leader—again, in a non-confrontational, positive way.

Helpful Hints

Many trainers who compete in performance events prefer teaching the *down* from the standing position, because it creates a faster *down* than going from a *sit* and then into a *down*.

The *down* is taught using a treat as a lure, similarly to the *sit*. You can begin with your dog in either a standing position or a sitting position for the *down*.

1. BEHAVIOR—Holding your Lab's collar loosely (just to keep him from backing up), and with your Lab either in a *sit* or standing, take a treat and pass it from his nose slightly backward toward his chest (if he's standing) and downward toward the floor. Do this slowly so that he folds himself downward into a *down* position. It's a bit tricky to get the positioning of the treat just right. You don't want him to bow to get the treat (or let his rump come up if he is in a *sit*).
2. COMMAND—Say "down" when your Lab is completely in a *down* with haunches, chest, and elbows all firmly on the floor.
3. MARK—REWARD—RELEASE—REPEAT.

ACTIVITIES For *Every* Lab

Activity	Type	Special Skills?	Organizations
Agility	Competitive	All Labs can benefit from this sport; those with joint problems will need to modify activity and may not be able to compete	American Kennel Club (AKC) Canine Performance Events Inc. (CPE) North American Dog Agility Council (NADAC) United Kennel Club (UKC) United States Dog Agility Association (USDAA)
Flyball	Competitive	Requires a team of four handlers and dogs; ability to jump low hurdles, catch and bring a ball back	North American Flyball Association (NAFA)
Musical Freestyle	Competitive	A little coordination, rhythm, and a willingness to dance with your dog to music	World Canine Freestyle Organization Musical Dog Sport Association
Obedience	Competitive	Good for ALL Labs; participate just to earn a title (pass/fail), or just have fun training	American Kennel Club (AKC) United Kennel Club (UKC)
Canine Good Citizen	Noncompetitive	Pass/Fail; tests dogs and handlers on basic skills that are beneficial to a well-behaved companion	American Kennel Club (AKC)
Rally	Noncompetitive	Pass/fail; ability to earn titles and have fun.	American Kennel Club (AKC) Association of Pet Dog Trainers (APDT)
Tracking	Noncompetitive	Pass/fail; requires some physical fitness from owner	American Kennel Club (AKC)
Animal Assisted Therapy	Noncompetitive; service	Rock solid temperament; training and certification through a national organization	The Delta Society Therapy Dogs International, Inc. R.E.A.D. (Reading Education Assistance Program)
Search and Rescue	Noncompetitive; service	Physically fit owner and dog; good tracking or trailing dog	National Association for Search and Rescue, Inc.

4. As your Lab begins to catch on, he will start lying down quickly the moment you start moving the treat. At this point, you can back up the command, "down," to when he is nearly in the *down*. As with the *sit* command, you will continue to make the exercise more difficult *gradually* by backing the command up to the point at which you will be standing in front of your Labby and can say "Down," and he will immediately lie down.

Come

The recall or *come* command is an important command for all Labs to know. Ideally, you'll never have to use it in a critical situation; however, if your Lab gets loose and begins bolting toward a busy road, it is comforting to know that the well-trained Lab will turn on a dime and return to you when you call him.

This type of recall does not happen overnight, and it does take a lot of work.

Helpful Hints

When calling your puppy or dog in from the backyard, condition the Lab to a hand clap or whistle toot. Link the signal with a treat just as you would the clicker. Avoid using the word "*come*" until you have reached a high level of proficiency with the command (i.e., your Lab never fails on a long line no matter what the distractions).

In fact, one of the key components of teaching this command is that you always work with your dog *on leash*. The reason for this is that you *never* want to give your Lab any inkling that the command "Come!" means anything *but* that he must come to you and come quickly.

If he's never had an opportunity to fail at this exercise, he won't fail you when it's critical—i.e., if you are in a position where you must use the command and your Lab is off leash. The *come* command can be worked on in a couple of different manners—and these techniques can be combined to increase the number of recall repetitions your Lab does in a day.

Method 1: While Walking

1. With your Lab on leash and while you are walking forward, suddenly start walking backward.
2. When your Lab hits the end of the leash, he will turn toward you to see what's going on.
3. Start trotting backward and encourage him to come toward you, saying his name or "Let's go" —but don't say *come* yet.
4. When your Lab is *actually trotting toward you*, say "Come!"
5. MARK—REWARD—RELEASE and continue on your walk.
6. REPEAT sporadically and without warning throughout your walking.
7. Make the exercise a little more difficult: As your Lab begins turning toward you, say "Come!" Then, the moment *you* change direction (and before your Lab realizes it), say "Come!"

Method 2: From the *Sit-Stay*

1. Put your Labby on a *sit-stay*. (He is to be on leash.)
2. Walk directly in front of him.
3. Say "Come!" as you trot backward. (Give the command the moment you start trotting backward, so he understands that it's okay for him to break his *sit-stay* command.)
4. MARK—REWARD—RELEASE—REPEAT.
5. Make the exercise more difficult by walking farther away from your Lab before you give him the command and trot backward.
6. Increase your distance from your Lab by using a long line used specifically for training this exercise. Always MARK—REWARD—RELEASE—REPEAT (eight to ten reps, although as always this can be broken up for puppies).

Walking Nicely on Leash

How many Lab owners have you seen being walked by their dogs? It's not that the Lab is a pushy dog; he's just strong, has a lot of energy, and wants to *go*. Your job is to teach him that if he walks nicely on a leash, he gets to go places . . . lots of places! It's easiest to teach good leash manners when a puppy is young. So if you've got a little guy, don't wait to work on walking your dog until he's a 60-pound adolescent. Start young and keep up the good work.

Here are the basics to teaching a Lab to walk nicely on leash:

1. Snap a leash onto your Lab's collar.
2. Begin walking.
3. Talk to him and tell him he's such a good boy! (This is marking the correct, loose leash behavior.) And give him a treat periodically to reward his good behavior.
4. If your Lab starts to go left, turn right.

5. The second he spins around to catch up to you, MARK—REWARD (you haven't given him a command per se, so he doesn't need a RELEASE command here).
6. The next time your Lab pulls ahead, turn around and walk in the opposite direction. Again, the second he turns around and tries to catch up to you, MARK—REWARD and continue with your walk.

This constantly changing movement will look a little funny to all who are watching you, and your neighbors may question your sanity; however, as your Lab catches on—and has perfect leash manners as a full-grown adult—you'll be grateful that you spent the time working with your pup, no matter how silly it looks in the early stages.

The Foundations of *Fetch*

What would owning a Labrador Retriever be like without being able to play fetch with your dog? The biggest problem owners have with *fetch* is that the Lab will fetch a ball or bumper only once and then he plays a game of keep-away. Whether you plan on hunting with your dog or simply want to be able to throw your dog a ball without him running off with it, it's important to make sure your Labby is never able to play "chase me."

The best way to do this is to begin all play sessions of fetch on a line. In this way, you can always reel in a wayward puppy. Throw the ball, allow the pup or dog to chase after it, and encourage him to return to you. You can play the game in a closed-in hallway at home—on a line—to make sure your puppy is even more likely to return the ball to you. **Note:** Do not use the command *come* when playing fetch. This is a game. *Come* is a command that you want your Lab to associate with coming to you immediately.

When your pup (or adult) returns with his prize, don't try to grab it from him immediately. Rub him down and praise him for being such a smart Lab,

and then ask for the ball. If he's really resistant to giving up his prize, offer him a treat. When he drops the ball for the treat, say "Out" and give him the treat. Young puppies should not be over-trained to fetch, particularly when they're young. In fact, top retriever trainers recommend that the game be played with potential hunting dogs a maximum of only three or four times a week with no more than two retrieves a session.

The natural drive to retrieve in the Lab does not require any encouragement, so the experts say that overdoing fetches at an early age doesn't help to build this drive. In fact, it can discourage the natural retrieving drive. By limiting the pup's retrieves, you are encouraging or heightening the excitement of getting to fetch, and you are making sure that *every* fetch is not only a huge event, but it is fun, exciting, and well-rewarded. Asking a pup to do multiple retrieves on a daily basis can bore a puppy with retrieves. And, perhaps most importantly, if a bored pup *doesn't* pick up the fetch toy and returns with nothing—this sets up the dog for unreliable retrieves for possibly the rest of his life.

Whether you plan to train your dog for hunting or not, be sure to stop the game before your Lab tires of retrieving the ball *or* before he becomes exhausted or overheated. Some Labs are so ball crazy that they will literally drop from heat or exhaustion before they'll stop bringing back the ball.

Leash Training

1 Begin by heading out on your walk.

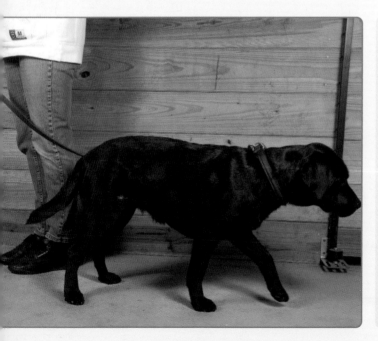

2 When your Labby chooses a direction other than the one you are headed in, *you* immediately turn in the opposite direction that your dog has chosen.

3 Oops! Gotta catch up! Encourage your Lab to hurry up and catch up.

4 Reward him when he walks with you on a slack leash.

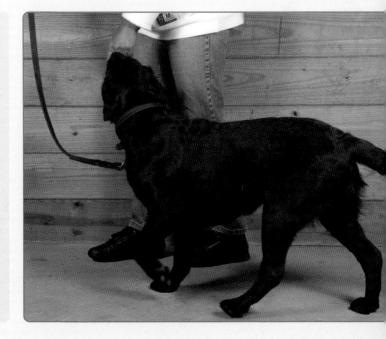

The *Sit* Command

1 With your dog's attention and a treat in hand, you can begin the *sit*.

2 Pass the treat slowly from his nose to the point behind his ears. He should naturally begin to fold his body into a *sit* as he follows the treat.

3 When he is fully in a *sit*, say "Sit!"

4 Mark the behavior with a "Yes!" or a <click>, and reward him with the treat.

The *Stay* Command

1 With your Lab in a *sit*, give him the hand signal for *stay* while saying "Stay."

2 Take a half step to the right, leading with your right foot.

3 Pause briefly and return immediately to your dog.

4 Mark the *stay* with "Yes!" and be sure to pat him on the chest to release him from the *sit-stay* after you've rewarded him with a treat or praise.

Chapter Eight

Grooming

T he Lab doesn't require the daily "hair care" ritual of a long-coated breed; however, Labs do need regular and thorough grooming. Though it's all pretty basic stuff, your Labrador's grooming will include not only coat care but also attention to his ears, teeth, and toenails.

How to Clip Nails

If there is one thing that *most* Lab owners agree on, it's that neither dog nor owner really enjoys the nail-trimming process. Nail trimming, however, is a necessary evil: Long nails can break and tear, they make it difficult to walk on slick floors, and lengthy talon-like nails cause a dog's paw to flatten unnaturally.

What makes nail clipping such a challenge for many dog owners is that Labs do not like to have their paws held. To get your dog to allow you to hold his paw and trim his nails may take quite a bit of practice. For this reason, it's important to practice trimming nails as often as possible as early as possible, and to keep the event *positive*.

Practice Makes Perfect

Obviously, you can't trim your Lab's nails every day, so part of the issue of acclimating your puppy or adult to nail clipping is that it's hard to get in practice time. Depending on how quickly your Labrador's nails grow, nail trimming could be a chore that's necessary every three to four weeks or every couple of months. Also, in the early stages of nail clipping, you're dealing with a wiggly puppy or possibly a very apprehensive adult dog, so you don't want

CAUTION

Better to Be Safe . . .

Paws can be "hot spots" for some rescued adult dogs, and an unknown dog may snap in fear when you touch his paws. Go slowly with a rescued Lab; remember, it will take time to build his trust in you.

to make a mistake. Don't make a big deal out of the event—treat it casually. If you say, "Oh, you poor dear," when your Lab puppy cries and tries to wriggle from your grasp, you've just confirmed to him that he *should* be trying to escape. Rather than confirm his suspicions, exude confidence by speaking and acting as if nail trimming is no big deal.

You want to ease your Lab into the event gradually. A way to solve the problem is through nail *taps*. When your Lab is fairly settled (i.e., about to fall asleep in your lap), gently hold a paw and tap a nail lightly with the clippers. Don't cut the nail yet. Give him a treat and praise him. Tap another nail lightly. Give him a treat and praise him again. See? This is a *fun* thing to do. Try to tap the nails on one paw at a session and then maybe two paws.

If after several days of the toe-tapping "game" your Lab is tolerating this touching exercise well, try to hold one of his paws a little longer. Don't get in an argument about it, but work on a getting a slightly longer "hold." Treat for good behavior and praise him!

While you're working on extending the light hold to a firmer paw grip, work to increase the toenail tap to a slight "grasp" with the clippers, as if you were trying to

Helpful Hints

What's Too Long?

If you can hear a faint "click" of the nails on pavement or a hard surface (i.e., tile floor, hardwood, etc.), the nails need to be trimmed.

BE PREPARED! Nail Clippers

When searching for a good nail clipper, look for a sharp, sturdy clipper that cuts the nail cleanly (a dull blade will crush the nail) in a scissors-like motion. Puppies can get by with a medium-weight clipper, but the adult Lab has such thick, tough nails, you'll eventually need to invest in the best, heavy-duty clipper you can find ($15–$25). Nail trimmers can sometimes leave jagged, sharp edges. To smooth out rough nail edges, you can use a sturdy nail file or a grinder that is made expressly for trimming and smoothing nails.

find the right place to clip the nail. Go from nail to nail and remember to praise and treat him for being a good boy.

Making the Actual Clip

Once your Labrador Retriever is comfortable with you holding his nails and the pressure of the nail clippers, trim a nail! If you've got a yellow Lab, you may have clear nails where you can actually *see* the pink-colored "quick," which is the blood supply of the nail.

To make the cut, hold the nail so you can see the side of it clearly. Place the clipper so that it is nearly to the tip of the quick. It is better to err on the side of making too little of a cut and trimming the nail a second time (or filing it) than to cut into the quick (it's a bloody mess, literally) or to get too close to the quick (some dogs are very sensitive and will react to a "near" quick).

If this trim goes well, continue with another nail *or* go back to holding the paw and simply "grasp" the other nails. Reward your Labby! He did really well. With puppies and adults, it's okay to trim one nail a day (if you can remember which nail you did) or one paw a day until the Labrador gets comfortable with nail trimming.

Remember, it's all about building positive, good experiences. If you don't quick him and he gets lots of treats and attention for being still, it won't be too long before he will tolerate nail trimming quite well.

Helpful Hints

Soften It Up!

If you are bathing your Lab, trim his toenails after you've washed him. Being in the water tends to soften the nail and can make your job a little easier.

The Dreaded Black Toenail

Oh, but wait. *Most* Labrador Retrievers don't have clear nails. They have solid black or mostly black nails. *This* is truly a challenge. You can't possibly see where the quick ends. There is a trick, however.

Turn your Lab's paw over so you can see the bottom of the nail. If you look closely, you will see an oval-shaped structure. This oval indicates where the quick is. To trim the black nail, look for this oval and make your cut slightly past it toward the nail tip. Once you have one nail cut, you can usually turn the paw back over and trim the same amount from each of the remaining nails.

Treating a Quicked Toenail

Ouch! You've done it! You quicked your puppy's nail. He's screaming. You're apologizing. And there's blood everywhere. Now what?

Stay calm and confident. Reach for your container of Quik Stop or another brand of powder that is sold to stop bleeding nails and dip the nail in the powder. If you don't have this product on hand, you can also use a styptic pencil (used by humans to stop shaving nicks). If all else fails, apply pressure with a cold washcloth until the nail clots (up to five minutes).

After treating the nail, and depending on how badly you cut into the quick, you'll need to keep your Lab quiet so he doesn't disturb the newly clotted nail. Putting him in his crate with a good chew or bone usually does the trick. When you continue trimming his nails (maybe later that day), arm yourself with treats and be prepared to go back to nail tapping and then gripping for a little while. He *may* be a bit jumpy, and understandably so.

Other Foot Care Tips

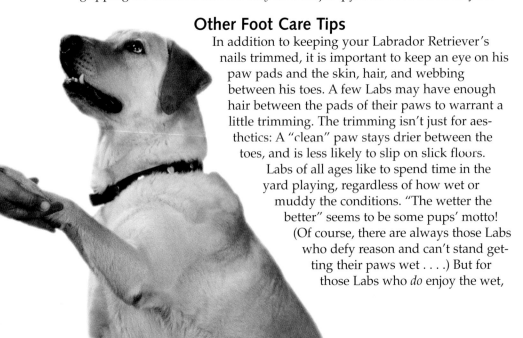

In addition to keeping your Labrador Retriever's nails trimmed, it is important to keep an eye on his paw pads and the skin, hair, and webbing between his toes. A few Labs may have enough hair between the pads of their paws to warrant a little trimming. The trimming isn't just for aesthetics: A "clean" paw stays drier between the toes, and is less likely to slip on slick floors. Labs of all ages like to spend time in the yard playing, regardless of how wet or muddy the conditions. "The wetter the better" seems to be some pups' motto! (Of course, there are always those Labs who defy reason and can't stand getting their paws wet . . . .) But for those Labs who *do* enjoy the wet,

HOME BASICS
Grooming

Coat	Brush: two–three times week; when shedding, brush daily	See "Grooming Tools" page on 134 for supplies
	Bathing: two–three times year	Dog shampoo; tearless and gentle on skin
	Rinsing: as needed	
Ears	Swab weekly; check for foreign bodies	Cotton ball moistened with clear water
	Smell for infection: weekly; inspect for excess wax	
	After-swim care	Drying agent as needed
	Ear canal hair care; pluck or trim *if* needed	
Nails	Trim every three to four weeks or as needed	Quality nail trimmer; nail file, or grinder, if desired; Quik Stop or styptic pen
Paws	Check pads and webbing weekly and after exercise	
	Dry after periods of wetness	Use a clean, dry towel
	Trim excess hair between pads of paws if needed	Personal trimmer or blunt-edged scissors
Teeth	Daily brushing	Finger brush or adult brush; dog toothpaste *only*
	Inspect mouth for injuries to teeth and gums; check for tumors.	
	Annual cleaning	Veterinary procedure that is performed under anesthesia

lay a towel down at the entrance to the back door and teach your pup or adult to *stand* on the towel while you wipe his feet. Be careful to wipe the spaces between his toes as dry as possible; this is an area that can become red, irritated, and sore if it remains wet for an extended time.

Winter snow and ice can also harm a puppy or adult dog's paws. After walks or other outdoor activities, be sure to clean the area between your Lab's toes and clear out any clumped snow, road salt or sand that might have accumulated there.

All About Teeth

According to the American Veterinary Dental Society, 80 percent of dogs show signs of oral and dental disease by the age of three. The good news: Labrador Retrievers have far better teeth than many other breeds, particularly toy breeds. The not-so-good news: Your Lab's teeth won't take care of themselves; they still require basic care from both you and your veterinarian to remain healthy well into old age.

The easiest way to keep your Lab's teeth and gums in good shape is to begin a canine dental hygiene program from the get-go. Basically, while your puppy is still agreeable, start brushing his teeth with a finger brush and doggie toothpaste. Use only toothpastes designed for dogs. Human toothpastes have chemicals in them that are harmful if swallowed—which is exactly what your Lab will try to do!

Finger brushes are not perfect, however:

1. They are knobby, made of rubber, and fit over your finger.
2. You will be coating this finger brush with doggie toothpaste that tastes like chicken or beef.
3. Your puppy *loves* to chew.

Breed Truths

Bad Breath?

Though a dog's bad breath is commonly a result of periodontal disease, it may also have another cause: kidney disease. Don't assume it's just "bad breath"; check it out with your veterinarian.

4 Your finger is going to be in his mouth.
5. The whole process resembles a great, new interactive chew toy to your puppy.
6. His teeth are like little, sharp needles and easily penetrate the rubber finger brush.

See the potential for problems here? Actually, it's not too bad. The first time you use the finger brush, try for a few swipes and then build up to a few back and forth motions on each side. Your goal is to acclimate your Lab to the brushing motion and to keep the tooth and gum line as clean as possible. As your Labby gets used to the finger brush, you can move to a larger, adult dog brush.

While you're brushing, be sure to keep an eye out for cavities that are affecting the dog, broken teeth, abscesses, and even tumors. If you spot any of these changes in your dog's mouth, see your veterinarian immediately.

In addition to daily brushing, your puppy or adult should avoid soft or sticky foods (diets are available that are made just for reducing tartar and

SHOPPING LIST

Grooming Tools

Grooming Tool	How It's Used	Approx. Cost
Pin Brush	To reach down into the undercoat and remove dead hairs; pins should have balls on the ends so as not to scratch the dog's skin	$5–$10
Short-haired Rake	Same purpose as the pin brush but can be used during high shedding seasons	$10–$15
Shedding Blade	A great tool for removing lots of dead hair quickly; be careful how hard you brush with this tool, as it can irritate sensitive skin	Large; $10–$12
Wire Slicker Brush	This will get the hair that the shedding blade or rake hasn't caught	Large; $15–$20
Zoom Groom	A rubber brush that helps loosen up dead undercoat and feels *great* on the dog's skin; also can be used during baths to clean deeply and loosen up even more hair; perfect for puppies, too	$10
FURminator	A rake-like tool that has a blade; very good at removing dead undercoat during high shedding seasons	$96 includes replacement blade
Bristle Brush	A good finishing brush to use with the direction of the hair; perfect puppy brush; distributes natural oils throughout coat; higher-quality bristles (boar) are more expensive	$5–$10 and up

calculus) and receive appropriate chewing toys. For additional care, ask your veterinarian if your Lab might benefit from a daily canine dental wash and/or a gel that can be applied to the surface of your dog's teeth and gums once a week.

Of course, even with the best dental home care, it's pretty near impossible to keep a dog's teeth perfectly clean. Because bacteria is released from

diseased gums and teeth into the dog's bloodstream (and affects internal organs), it's important to schedule routine dental cleaning with your veterinarian. It's not inexpensive because the process does require your Lab to be under general anesthesia; however, if you schedule his cleaning on an annual basis—and you are vigilant in your home cleaning—the costs will be less.

Breed Truths

Owners who do their own grooming and who are very hands-on with their Labs are much more likely to spot potential problems, such as skin conditions (i.e., a hidden hot spot), injuries, pests, and even disease in its earliest stages.

Brushing

Many people purchase a loveable, plush Labrador Retriever puppy only to discover that, oh, around seven to nine months when the pup's adult coat starts to come in, the Labrador *sheds*.

And, it's not just losing a puppy coat that causes copious amounts of hair. There's daily shedding and seasonal sheds, too.

HOME BASICS
Shedding: It's the Seasons!

Spring and fall are high shedding seasons. In the spring, your Lab will lose much of his undercoat and a lot of his guard hairs, too. In the fall, *everything* sheds out as the denser winter undercoat comes in along with a new top coat. During these times you will wonder how your Labrador can possibly still have any hair on his body after cleaning up all the hair on your floors and furniture!

To control shedding as best as possible *groom every day*. Use a shedding blade or rake, or a specialty shedding product, such as the FURminator. Brush with the lay of the hair to remove as much dead hair as possible. Do this outside and stand upwind of your dog!

No kidding. Piles of hair will come out on a daily basis. You don't want this all over you!

Follow up with a pin brush, working backward through your dog's coat first, and then with the lay of the hair to finish. Don't even bother pulling out the bristle brush; it will fill up too quickly to be of much use at this point.

Bathe your dog during this time to help remove even more hair. Use a good rubber scrubber such as the Zoom Groom to help get down to the undercoat and wash out as much dead hair as humanly possible. Dry thoroughly and go through the brushing regimen again, and again, and again.

So, how do you get around all this hair? Basically, you can attack it when it hits the floor (i.e., if you don't have a good vacuum cleaner, invest in one), or you can go directly to the source: your Labrador. Thoroughly brushing your dog from head to toe at least two to three times a week will go far in limiting the amount of hair you'll need to vacuum from your floors and upholstery. Your Lab will still shed in the house; it just won't be quite as much.

Regular brushing also has added benefits. The time you spend grooming your Lab is a pleasant experience for him. In fact, not only does the brushing feel good to your Lab, but it helps to improve his circulation and makes for a healthier, shinier coat. But even beyond that, quiet moments like this with your dog are truly bonding experiences.

The Simple Art of Brushing

Part of the reason the Labrador Retriever sheds so much is that he is a double-coated breed. The Labrador has a soft, downy undercoat and a coarser, sturdy outer coat that is made of guard hairs. You will find both types of hair in your home. Usually the undercoat accumulates on slick, hard floors in wafty piles, whereas the coarser guard hairs expertly lodge themselves in upholstery.

To brush your Lab, begin with a pin brush. Brush with the direction of the coat to warm up your Lab to his brushing session. Then, begin working at

the base of his tail, and in short, brisk strokes brush his entire coat backward. You'll want to make sure that the brush pins work down to his skin.

Be careful not to "dig" with the brush; you want your Lab to feel like he's getting a back scratch, not a torture session!

The hair should be flying at this point—oh, you'll probably want to do this outside, by the way. Once you've worked the coat against the lay of the hair, go back over the entire coat *in the same direction as the hair*. You can finish up your grooming session with a softer, bristle-type brush (which helps distribute the natural oils in your dog's coat) and finally, wipe with a damp towel to pick up any loose or stray hair.

Bathing and Drying

The Labrador Retriever is the ultimate gundog, and as such he has a classic "gundog" coat. The oily coat sheds water and helps retain heat when in cold water.

Helpful Hints

Ewwww! Dandruff!

Dogs can get dandruff, too. It's commonly found around the base of the tail, neck, and back. Flaky skin can be the result of the Lab's diet, or a shampoo that wasn't rinsed out very well, or it could indicate the onset of a skin infection, high stress levels, allergies, or parasites. To determine how to treat flaky skin, you'll need to have your veterinarian determine the cause.

The Labrador's coat can also smell. This distinct odor is most observable after swimming or a hard run outside. The smell generally dissipates as the Lab dries or cools down from the outdoors. Sometimes, however, it will be

BE PREPARED! Spotting Early Signs of Disease

Body Part	How to Examine	What to Feel or Look For
Skin	Pressing gently, feel and palpate the entire surface of your Lab's skin	Lumps and bumps under the surface of the skin; possibly fatty tumors (relatively harmless) or signs of a more aggressive tumor
	Part hair with hands or look carefully as you brush backward during grooming sessions	Irritated, raw, or infected patches of skin that could be "hot spots" caused from parasites, injury, itching or scratching
	Using a fine-tooth comb, brush through areas behind ears and at the base of the tail	Look for tiny bits of dark dirt like specks on the skin that could be a sign of fleas
Teeth	Gently pull back lips; observe changes in breath	Inflamed gums, bleeding, plaque deposits on teeth, broken or cracked teeth, unusual growths or no signs of disease but persistent bad breath
Ears	Lift the ear flap for visual inspection; smell ear	Redness, inflammation, warmth, dark or reddish wax, offensive smell; head shaking, rubbing, scratching
Eyes	Visual inspection	Tearing or watery eyes, discharge, inflammation, redness, obvious discomfort
Paws	Visual inspection	Cracked pads, redness between pads, torn nails, inflammation

necessary to bathe your Lab. Labradors should be bathed only every two to three months—unless they've gotten into something particularly ripe that necessitates an *immediate* washing. Too much bathing will remove too much of the coat's oils, drying out the skin and causing the outer coat to become dull and brittle.

When you do bathe your Lab, make sure you use lukewarm water—not too hot and not too cold. A bathtub works best with a spray nozzle that can be attached to the showerhead or tub faucet. Be sure to put a rubber nonslip pad in the base of the tub to keep your dog from slipping.

Wet your Lab thoroughly, avoiding his ears and eyes. (You can use a washcloth for these areas.) Once you've gotten him wet—and it can be a chore trying to completely soak that undercoat because your Lab is so water-resistant—apply a high-quality dog shampoo and work it in. Use a rubber brush, such as the Zoom Groom, to help remove excess undercoat and scrub out dirt that has really worked its way down to the skin.

Once you've really scrubbed your Lab, wash out all the shampoo. When you think you've gotten all the shampoo out and the water is running clear, rinse him all over again. Any remnant of shampoo in his coat will cause him to itch later.

After your second full rinse, make sure all the water in the tub has drained and rinse his legs and paws *one more time*. Because the dog is often standing in a few inches of water during a bath, it is common to have a little soap still in his legs and paws after a bath. Rinse, rinse, rinse!

Helpful Hints

Shampoos

There are shampoos for black coats and light coats, sensitive skin and sensitive eyes, to put shine in and to fluff coats out. So many choices! What do you use? Start with a good, tearless dog shampoo that is made for the pH level of a dog's skin.

Drying Time

Ideally you have a stack of dry towels at the ready *and* you've remembered to shut the door to the bathroom *firmly*. If not, you'll have a grand time chasing your wet Lab as he bounds over, under, and through everything in your home with the "I've-got-the-after-bath zoomies." Good luck!

When you *do* catch your Lab, towel him as dry as possible. Crate him with warm bedding in an area in the home without breezes or drafts until he is dry. If you prefer, you *can* blow-dry your dog. If you do use a blow dryer, use one made for dogs. Or if you use a "human" blow dryer, put the setting on "cool." Blow dryers for humans heat up too much for a dog's skin.

Don't forget to dry your dog's ears, too, with an ear wash or rinse. These products help to remove excess wax, debris, and water while cleaning the ear canal. Your veterinarian can provide you with good choices for this.

Fun Facts

Dog Washes

During high shedding periods, consider using a local dog wash for $15–$20. It costs less than a groomer, and all the shampoos and tools are provided. Best of all, you don't have to deal with cleaning up all the wet hair afterward.

Ear Maintenance

Common sources of ear infections include an injury (scratch or cut), or the presence of a foreign body (such as a foxtail) in the ear canal. Also, rather than sneezing, itching, and getting watery eyes, dogs often respond to inhaled, ingested, or contact allergens by developing serious recurrent ear infections.

To keep your Lab's ears healthy, inspect them regularly. And, though it sounds rather odd, sniff your dog's ears. One of the first signs of an ear infection is a horrid, rank odor. If you're well versed in what a healthy Lab's ears smell like, you'll *know* when something is amiss.

CAUTION

Ouch! Whatcha Doin?

If you have adopted an adult dog, approach his ears gently. If he has had an ear infection in the past, he may react as if he's in severe pain. The memory of pain lasts much longer than the tenderness itself.

Also, use a cotton ball to wipe away any dirt that may have accumulated in the crevices of your dog's ears. Don't use a swab, as this can damage the ear canal. Be on the lookout for any redness, inflammation, blood, and/or excessive wax. Dark, waxy secretions are *not* normal for most dogs and warrant a trip to the veterinarian's office for a check.

If your Lab does a lot of swimming (and comes in contact with all the muck and bacteria that can be in

stagnant water), or if he is prone to ear infections for other reasons, ask your veterinarian about the possibility of using an ear wash or rinse. These rinses can help to dislodge foreign debris and trapped swamp water, and help to keep the appropriate yeast levels constant.

Another sign of ear problems is head shaking, scratching, holding the head at an odd angle, or an increased sensitivity to touch. If you suspect an infection, seek veterinary treatment for your Lab immediately. Left untreated, ear infections can cause permanent, lasting damage.

The Eyes Have It

Your Labrador's eyes should be clear, bright, and free of any "gook." Most puppies and dogs won't have any residue in their eyes; however, if there's an occasional bit of residue, a quick swipe with a moistened cotton ball is all that's needed.

If you find that your Lab's eyes are constantly gooey in the morning, if the whites of the eyes are reddened, or if there's obvious inflammation or excessive weeping or tearing, take your dog to the veterinarian for an exam. There are many causes for some of these symptoms, ranging from allergies and injuries, to an inward-turning eyelash or a hereditary eye disease.

Regardless of the cause, if the eye is uncomfortable for the puppy or dog, he's going to rub and scratch at it and cause further injury. Get him to the veterinary office to have the problem checked out immediately.

Chapter Nine

The Senior Labrador Retriever

T he silver sheen on the muzzle of an aging Labrador is the hallmark of a life well lived. Genetics certainly play a role in a dog's potential life span; however, if you have the privilege of owning a senior Lab, that fact that he has lived so long and so well is testament to your level of care and concern. As many owners discover, it's not necessarily expensive surgeries or medicines that keep our aging pets comfortable, but a little understanding, ingenuity, and the willingness to adapt our homes and lives just a little for those final years.

Enriching an Older Dog's Life

Too often owners assume that because their Labs are sleeping all day and reluctant to move from the couch, this lifestyle is what makes them happiest. To prove this theory wrong, pick up the dog's leash and say, "Wanna go for a walk?" and see what happens.

Chances are those very words will take *years* off your Lab's current age and transform him back to near puppyhood. The eyes will light up. That big rope of a tail will begin swinging, and even if it's now an effort, he'll hoist himself off the couch and trot over to you, pushing his big head into your hands so you can snap on the leash.

Just because he doesn't demand a lot of your attention anymore doesn't mean that he doesn't still need interaction and stimulation to maintain good health. In fact, offering your Labrador a life "enriched" with stimulating activities is crucial to maintaining his physical as well as mental health.

Enrichment 101

So, how can you enhance your Labrador's senior years? It's really pretty easy. Actually, many of the "enriching" activities are the very things you used to do when your Lab was younger to keep him out of trouble.

Exercise Remember those thrice-daily, 30-minute, vigorous walks or bicycling routes you used to take with your Labrador when he was younger? (If you forgot a walk, he bounced and ran and annoyed you until you

FYI: How Old Is Old?

In 2006, a panel of experts was asked to develop veterinary care guidelines for senior dogs for the American Animal Hospital Association; however, the panel found it could not define geriatric. Every breed, every dog, is different. Generally speaking, a nine-year-old Labrador is considered "older," and when a dog hits seven or eight years, owners should be on the lookout for subtle changes.

did take him for his romps.) Gentle exercise for shorter distances—let him set the speed—will benefit his heart, lungs, circulation, and joints. Additionally, the sights, sounds, and smells he will encounter on his walks are mentally stimulating.

Take Him with You Though he may only open one eye and gently thump his otter tail on the couch when you pick up the car keys, that doesn't mean he doesn't want to come with you. If he's good in the car, bring him along. In fact, take him everywhere you possibly can and that he's comfortable going. The change of scenery is good for him, the sights and sounds are mentally interesting, and the extra rides give him even more time with you.

Touch Him When he was younger, your Labrador was likely only a step or two away from you at all times. He got a lot of pats back then, didn't he? Now he's often on his bed and not underfoot, but he will benefit just as much—if not more—from physical attention as a senior. Make time to give him rubs and pats, maybe a nice massage, and (even if he doesn't need it) daily grooming.

Talk to Him He loves the sound of your voice, truly. Tell him about your day, explain to him what you're cooking, discuss future vacation plans. It doesn't really matter what you're talking about, he'll enjoy the conversation and companionship.

Teach Him New Things Labs never stop learning. Older dogs enjoy the time and hands-on attention they get when they're being taught a new

ACTIVITIES Therapy Anyone?

An older Lab that is calm, well mannered, and *loves* people could excel in animal-assisted therapy work or might make an *outstanding* "reading" partner for a young child as part of an animal-assisted reading program. Check out the opportunities in your area!

skill, command, or trick. Be aware of what his physical limitations are (i.e., folding into a *sit* or rising from a *down* may be a little painful) and select activities that he'll enjoy.

Introduce Him to New, Friendly People and Dogs If your Lab was always the life of the dog park or enjoyed afternoons at the kids' soccer games, even though he's older (or your kids are now in college) he will still enjoy making new human and canine friends. Seek out "quiet" dog park times (when the wild youngsters aren't around) or set up a "senior" play group with other aging Lab friends. Take him back to his old stomping grounds at the soccer fields and let him make new kid friends. If he enjoyed being the center of attention before, it's likely he'll think it's great now, too.

Give Him Interactive Toys Yes, they make toys that require a dog to solve problems. These toys are great for puppies because they keep them occupied, but they serve as mental stimulation for older dogs, too!

Love Him He's a treasured, well-loved pet. You'll miss him when he's gone, so make sure you have no regrets *now*. Give him the attention he deserves and so loves.

Breed Needs

Creature Comforts

Older dogs often become chilled easily. Make sure your aging Lab's bedding is thick and deep, and his bed is indoors, out of the way of drafts or cold air. You might also consider a sweater or jacket to cut the chill when out on walks.

Hint: If you find the selection at pet stores and boutiques too frou-frou for your dog (and you), check out a local tack shop for horse-blanket-type dog jackets. They're handsome and practical, too.

Regular Checkups

In addition to keeping your Lab's life enriched, it's important to keep up on his health, too. Many owners dread going to the veterinarian's office because they fear "bad" news; however, the truth is that many conditions, if caught early, can be treated or managed well, giving an older Labrador *years* of healthy, high-quality living.

Because changes can come about quickly as a dog ages, experts recommend that an older Lab actually have more frequent veterinary "well" exams—at least two exams a year.

Hands-on Ownership (How to Keep a Close Eye on Changes)

You are your aging Lab's first line of defense. You know your dog better than anyone else. If you are very hands-on with your Lab on a daily basis, you're likely to detect subtle changes that can be important to address to maintain your Lab's good health and quality of living.

BE PREPARED! Establishing What's Normal *Now*

To establish what is healthy or considered normal for your dog *before* he shows signs of illness or disease, it is likely that your veterinarian will ask to have some baseline blood work performed.

Baseline Tests			
Test	**What It Is**	**Looking for**	**Indicates**
Complete Blood Cell Count (CBC)	Red and white blood cell count	Abnormally high numbers of white cells; abnormally low numbers of red cells	Possible infection, disease, anemia
Blood Chemistry Profile	A test that looks for the presence of other things in the blood	Proteins, electrolytes, glucose, cholesterol, potassium, chloride, etc.	Early indicators of disease or change in the functioning abilities of the liver, kidney, and pancreas; health of muscles and bone
Urinalysis	A study of the dog's urine that looks at the composition and contents	pH value, presence of crystals, blood, proteins, etc.	Signs of fever, dehydration, disease, and infection

Some changes that are typical with older dogs include the following:

Skin As a dog ages, he may have decreased circulation, which can cause his skin to be drier and more sensitive. Brushing his coat daily will help to improve skin circulation, increase oil production, and spread these oils more evenly throughout his coat.

Look for flakiness, which could be a sign of other health conditions or parasites. Also, part the hair and look for early signs of "hot spots," areas of irritation or infection of the skin. Causes for hot spots vary, but regardless, they are uncomfortable and need to be treated.

Feel for lumps and bumps. If you find any growth *anywhere* on your dog, have your veterinarian check it out immediately. The Labrador Retriever is predisposed to the development of lipomas (benign fatty tumors), as well as many different kinds of cancer. (See "Cancers," page 95 and "Lipomas," page 96 for more information.)

Nails An aging dog's nails need to be kept short in order to avoid slipping on slick floors. A fall on a slick floor can injure a senior dog; an arthritic dog may not be able to get up on his own. Aging nails can be drier or more crumbly, so make sure that your nail clipper is sharp, and file rough edges.

Teeth If your Lab is having difficulties eating or is not wolfing his food down as robustly as usual, he could be experiencing tooth or gum pain. Keep up the cleaning (see pages 132–135) and visually inspect your Lab's gums and teeth on a regular basis.

Changes in Appetite It is thought that an aging dog may gradually lose his sense of taste, so it may be necessary to change your dog's food to a more highly palatable food (one that tastes better). Other ways to improve your senior's appetite are to warm his food, and to make it wetter (a lot of dogs like their food sloppy) with something über enticing, such as low-salt chicken or beef broth.

If you see that your Lab isn't digesting his food as well (much of it passes right through him), it is possible that he is having greater difficulty metabolizing his food and isn't extracting necessary nutrients. Make sure you are feeding him a high-quality food that is nutrient packed. For advice on choosing the best food currently available on the market for your dog—and to make sure his increasing amount of stool is not related to another factor entirely—consult with your veterinarian.

CAUTION

Laryngeal Paralysis

The full or partial collapse of a dog's larynx is a potentially fatal condition that often occurs among elderly Labs. Symptoms include
- panting, difficulty breathing
- hoarse-sounding bark
- gagging, coughing
- exercise intolerance
- fainting

Depending on the serverity of the condition, medications may help or surgery may be required.

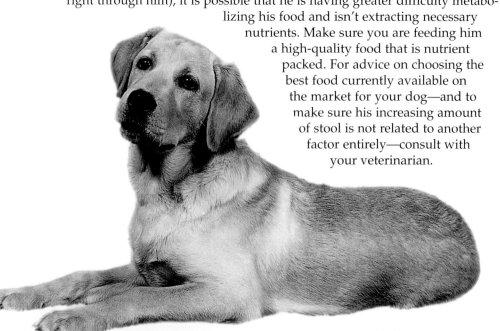

Managing Incontinence (For Girls . . . Mostly)

If your Labrador has been picture perfect when it comes to her house training and she's suddenly having "accidents," it could be because of incontinence. Typically, incontinence occurs when the urinary sphincter has become weakened. It is quite common among spayed female Labs and less frequent (but not impossible) among males.

Incontinence is different than "having accidents" in that the incontinent Labrador is *unaware* that she is urinating. Leaks often occur when the Lab is sound asleep, but it can also happen when she's awake and relaxing in her bed. Incontinence can occur sporadically (with days or even months of dryness between leaks) *or* a dog may regularly experience multiple leaks every day.

Before assuming that wet spots in the house are the result of incontinence, have your veterinarian examine your Lab. Wetting could be a symptom of other diseases, such as a urinary tract infection, diabetes, kidney disease, or a thyroid condition.

Helpful Hints

Clean and Dry

Wrap your dog's bed in a garbage or yard bag and then zip the bed's cover over the plastic-wrapped bed. If there's a leak, you can wash the outer cover and replace the plastic bag.

Changes That Can Help the Incontinent Lab

Losing weight can sometimes solve an incontinence problem. A dog that carries excess weight puts more pressure on the bladder, which in turn puts more pressure on the urinary sphincter.

Exercise can also help—not only in helping with weight control but also in giving more muscular support in the sphincter area.

Developing a routine can be very beneficial to the incontinent Lab: Make sure you pick up her water 30 minutes before bedtime and allow her to void completely before she turns in for the night. The more she empties her bladder, the less pressure will be on the urinary sphincter.

And, if your Lab *does* leak, wash the urine thoroughly from her coat. If left in her coat, the urine will not only smell awful, but can also burn her skin. For big accidents, wash the affected area with a mild hypoallergenic shampoo and towel-dry. For little leaks, a baby wipe can be used.

Veterinary Intervention

If the incontinence is regular and affecting the dog's (and your) quality of life, consult with your veterinarian about the use of prescription medications. These medications have a high to total success rate and are available with minimal side effects.

In those few cases in which medications are not effective, surgery may be an option. In cases in which all other therapies have failed, collagen injections have been used with some success to narrow the urinary sphincter.

Coping with Blindness and Deafness

If you suspect that your Labrador may be going blind or deaf, consult with your veterinarian. Though hearing *does* deteriorate over time and aging Labradors *can* have decreased vision caused by natural, age-related clouding of the eye (nuclear sclerosis), it is advisable not to assume anything.

If you find that your Labrador's vision or hearing is impaired and there's nothing that can be done to improve his condition, take heart! There are many things that you can do to help him live comfortably in your home.

Vision Impaired

For Labbies that don't see so well, it's important to keep your furniture in place and pick up your floors. Try to keep shoes in the closet, packages up on tables, and purses or bags out of high-traffic areas.

Vision-impaired dogs can often get confused if they walk behind an open door and can't figure out why they can't get through the opening. Leave a scent trail (a spray bottle with a *very* dilute scent works nicely) that makes a path through your home, including doorways, to help prevent the blind Lab from getting stuck or confused.

Also, ask visitors and friends to allow the blind dog to approach them (rather than reaching down to pet the dog on the head). With limited or no vision, the sudden touch of a hand can be startling to the aging Labrador. For more information on working with a blind dog, visit *www.blinddogs.com*.

Hearing Impaired

Typically, Labradors adjust very well to the loss of hearing in one ear. In fact, they compensate so well that owners typically won't notice that the dog has any hearing loss until the deficit is in *both* ears.

The biggest problem with bilateral hearing loss is that the Lab simply doesn't hear you. Startling (particularly while sleeping) can be a new behavioral problem for dog owners, as a dog's typical response to a serious fright is snapping.

To wake your dog more gently, teach him a new "alert" signal. This can be stomping on the floor or using a vibrating collar. When your Lab is awake but not looking at you, stomp on the floor or activate the vibration in the collar. When he turns to look at you, reward him with praise and a treat. What a good boy! As he learns that the stomp or buzz means for him to look at you, it is safe to use this alert system when he's sleeping, too.

Fun Facts

DIY Electric Collars

Instructions for making a collar for a hearing-impaired dog (along with a complete listing of retail vibrating collars and prices) can be found at *www.deafdogs.org* under "vibe collars." The project involves a film canister, an inexpensive (tiny) electric car, and a little MacGyver-type know-how.

Working with Cognitive Dysfunction Syndrome (CDS)

A definite concern among owners of older Labs is whether their dogs will become senile. The loss of cognitive function or cognitive dysfunction syndrome (CDS) is not uncommon. One study indicated that 18 percent of pet owners of dogs aged seven years or older noted at least one clinical sign of the disease. By the time the dog was 11 years or older, 28 percent of pet owners noticed at least one sign of CDS; many owners saw multiple symptoms of the disease.

Treatment of CDS

Once the possibility of other diseases or conditions has been ruled out, the treatment goal for CDS is to slow the progression of cognitive loss. This can be achieved in many ways.

Diet A therapeutic food (Hill's Prescription Diet b/d) that contains antioxidants, such as alpha-lipoic acid, beta-carotene, and vitamin C; and fish-based omega-3 fatty acids, such as docosahexaenoic acid (DHA) and eicosapentaenoic acid (EPA), has shown signs of improving cognitive abilities in older dogs. Check with your veterinarian for updates on research on this and other promising foods and/or supplements as they become available.

Prescription Medications ANIPRYL (Selegiline hydrochloride, L-deprenyl) has a good track record of helping many dogs with CDS and has been shown to temporarily reverse and improve behaviors in some dogs within 30 days. The drug is also available by prescription in a generic form.

BE PREPARED! Four Symptoms of CDS

CDS can present many different symptoms, but these four are the most commonly seen early signs:

Symptom	Description of Behaviors
Disorientation	A dog (that is not blind) stands behind the hinged side of a door and seems confused about why he can't walk into the next room
Variances in social behaviors	A people-loving Lab suddenly doesn't want to greet known friends, is confused by strangers, or is less happy to greet his owner; a dog-friendly Lab is aggressive or shy with former playmates
Interrupted sleep cycle	Sleeping more in the day and less at night; waking up at night and pacing and panting for no apparent reason (i.e., dog is not arthritic or uncomfortable for other reasons)
Loss of house training	Dog appears to be confused with where he can relieve himself; underlying diseases and causes ruled out

Mental Stimulation The old adage of "Use it or lose it" seems to apply to a dog's mental health as well as a human's. Ways to "use it" include walks around the neighborhood, which stimulate all of a dog's senses and helps to get his mind working. Interaction with friendly people and dogs is a good mental exercise (*if* he is still friendly and confident), and offering your aging Lab fun, problem-solving toys (in which he has to work to get the treats to release) or hiding familiar toys in unusual places are other good ways to mentally stimulate your Lab. And of course, light, positive, reward-based obedience work and trick training can go a long way toward helping to keep an older dog's mind as active as possible.

Confidence Helps

Your attitude, tone of voice, and overall confidence can be one of the most influential forces on an aging Lab suffering from arthritis. If *you* take a "can-do" approach (as opposed to a pitying, I-feel-so-sorry-for-you, consoling manner), your Lab will be much more confident and happier. Remember, if you're worried, so is he.

Easing Arthritis

A fact of life of owning a larger, heavier breed of dog, such as the Labrador Retriever, is that osteoarthritis is going to affect his joints at some point. Everyday use wears away at the cartilage or natural cushioning in a dog's joints, particularly his hips, elbows, and knees. If a dog has sustained an injury, has a disease (i.e., hip dysplasia), or is overweight, the cartilage in the joint may wear down faster than that of a slim dog with a good build and healthy joints.

Regardless of the factors involved in how quickly the cartilage wears down, once it's gone, it's gone. Movement in a joint with little cartilage causes severe pain and inflammation. Unfortunately, by the time you detect a slight limp in your Labrador's gait, he could already be suffering from severe degenerative arthritis with little hope of improving the joint through moderate methods.

Once There's Pain

If your Lab is already showing signs of arthritis (X-rays of the joints can confirm problem areas), you'll still want him to exercise (motion *is* lotion to the joints); however, you'll need to keep the exercises less strenuous. If you have a pool, an animal-therapy pool, or access to a clean body of water, swimming is a wonderful means of exercise for the arthritic dog—if the water isn't too cold!

In addition to gentle, regular exercise, there are many other helpful ways to assist your Labrador and help him feel more comfortable.

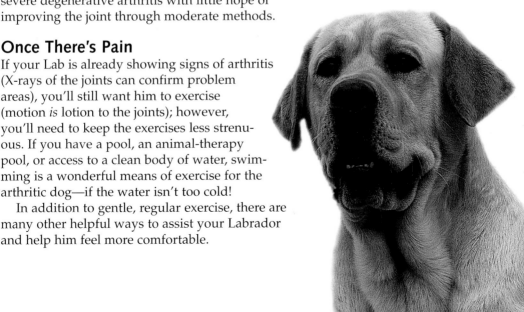

HOME BASICS
Arthritis Pain

Lying in one position can be painful for the arthritic dog. Several different types of pads are available, most of which are made to take pressure off the joints by providing *supportive* bedding; however, there are some gel-type pads that have cooling properties, too.

Walking on slick floors is difficult with stiff and sore joints. To prevent painful slips, keep his nails short and provide solid footing throughout the house with carpeting, rugs, and rubber pathways on hard floors. Also, consider using a sling/harness, so that when he has difficulties getting up from the floor, you can grab the handle on the harness and give him assistance.

Bending down to eat dinner from a bowl on the floor can be a challenge for the arthritic dog. Raise food and water bowls so they are more easily accessible.

And finally, the simple joys, such as jumping up on the bed to sleep with you or hopping into the car, can now be extremely painful. Portable ramps and steps can be used to allow your Lab to walk into the car and continue to snuggle up in bed with you at night.

No Extra Pounds Obesity is an *enormous* (no pun intended) problem with adult Labrador Retrievers. Every excess pound is an additional four pounds of pressure on his joints. If he's hurting from arthritis, he doesn't need any extra weight! If your Labrador isn't already slim and trim, you need to help him shed some weight.

Joint Supplements Supplements such as glucosamine HCL, chondroitin sulfate, and methyl sulfonylmethane (MSM) are often prescribed to be added to a dog's diet. Though some study results have been conflicting on the effectiveness of these supplements, other studies have shown some promise as to the substances' ability to reduce arthritic pain and improve the condition of the joint. Some high-quality foods are being produced with these supplements in the ingredients.

Prescription Medications When diet, regular, light exercise, and the addition of supplements are not enough to ease your Labrador's arthritic pain, prescription medications may be beneficial. Non-steroidal anti-inflammatory drugs (NSAID) have been shown to be very effective in reducing joint inflammation and improving mobility and comfort in the arthritic dog.

NSAIDs *do* have side effects, however. Labrador Retrievers, in particular, seem to have more adverse reactions than other breeds to at least one popular NSAID. Until it is known if Labs have an increased risk of side effects from NSAIDs, practice caution when considering adding an NSAID to your Labrador's arthritis care plan. Talk over the risks completely and thoroughly with your veterinarian and make your decision based on the best possible data available at that time.

Veterinarians will often honor Internet prices for costly arthritis medications and supplements if you print out your online order (with shipping and tax totals). Or, if this is not possible, ask your veterinarian for your dog's prescriptions and order his medications online from a trusted vendor.

CAUTION

Careful with Supplements

Any supplement that has the capacity to have a positive effect on a dog can also have the capacity to have an adverse effect, so it's advisable to discuss doses and brands of supplements with your veterinarian before "self-medicating" your Lab.

Surgical Options

In some cases, your veterinarian may suggest one or more surgical measures to provide your arthritic Lab with some pain relief. Surgeries can range from arthroscopy (a minimally invasive operation to remove loose bits in the joint or to smooth out cartilage), fusion (in which one bone is fused to another), or a partial or total joint replacement. The type of surgery that might be recommended for your dog depends on the specific joint and the amount of degeneration present.

Whether surgery is actually a viable option for your Lab depends on many factors, including the dog's overall health, his age, your financial ability to pay for such an operation, *and* your physical ability to care for a large-breed dog during his convalescence and rehabilitation.

If your veterinarian recommends surgery, discuss its pros and cons, making sure the surgeon addresses all of your concerns and questions. You will want to make sure that the potential for a good outcome far outweighs the risks and pain associated with the surgery and recovery from the operation.

Are You on the Same Page?

How far do you want to go to save your pet? To manage a chronic disease? To treat a terminal illness? Before your Labrador Retriever becomes ill, make sure that you and your veterinarian are on the same page. There's nothing worse than getting to a point at which you *know* your Lab has had enough and it's time to let go, and having your veterinarian want to try another expensive procedure. Or, *you* want to try another treatment option and your veterinarian thinks euthanasia is appropriate. Only you really know what your Lab's quality of life is and what it will be. Determining how far you want to go is much easier to decide when your dog is healthy, and will help to ensure that when the toughest decisions have to be made, you and your veterinarian are in agreement.

Chapter Ten

For Labradors Especially

One of the most profoundly satisfying activities for a Lab owner is working a dog in an activity for which he has been bred to excel—and watching the lightbulb go on. The pure joy with which these dogs perform on land and in water is simply breathtaking and something every owner should be able to share with their Labs.

Beginning Strategies for Future Hunters

You're watching your Lab puppy play and you're thinking, hmm . . . I wonder if he could hunt . . . Beginning, basic training for retrievers doesn't usually begin until a dog is six months old. However, if you're considering dabbling in the retrieving world, there are several exercises you can be doing with your Lab puppy before sending him to a professional trainer or beginning his formal training yourself with a good hunt club.

Retrieving With your pup on a line, throw a bumper down a carpeted hallway in your home. (Avoid slick floors, as any slipping, even as a puppy, can cause injuries with lasting effects.) Make sure he always returns the fetch toy to you. Don't ask him to let go of his prize immediately; make big over him for a while and he'll give it to you himself. If he's determined not to give it to you, offer him a treat (keep some in your pocket) and swap the treat for the ball.

Helpful Hints

Search for local and regional clubs on the LRC's Web site under "About LRC" and "Regional Clubs" at *www.thelabradorclub.com*.

Play this game only two to three times a week with no more than two retrieves a session. Also, never play tug-of-war with a future gundog! Your Lab will want to play tug at the most inopportune times, such as when he's just retrieved a pheasant to you in a hunt test.

Social Skills Work on your Lab puppy's social skills with people. You'll want him to be friendly and comfortable in crowds of people and with other dogs.

Recalls Begin working on your Lab's *come*, but make sure it's always on-line and you always make it as exciting as possible for him to *run* to you.

General Obedience Don't neglect to work on *sit, down,* and *stay.* These skills will be important later in his gundog training.

Gunfire You want your pup to associate good things with muzzle blasts. It is critical, however, that you begin this training *slowly* and at a distance. And, do not start with any type of gunfire. Begin by slapping two blocks of wood together roughly 20 feet away from where your pup is eating. Work up to slapping the blocks of wood closer, if he doesn't show any signs of reacting negatively to the sound.

Gentle Water Introduction Do not toss your puppy into the pool. This will not teach him to swim or to enjoy water. Introduce him to water slowly and always keep him on a line so you can reel him back in. (You don't want to allow "free" swims during which your pup could learn you can't catch him if he's in the water.) Another Lab that likes water is a great incentive for the puppy to join in the fun.

Doing What Comes Naturally . . .

If training your Lab to hunt or to participate in hunting activities interests you, there are many activities and sports you can enjoy with him that will bring out *his* natural talents. If you've never fired a shotgun before (and don't want to), that's not a problem for many hunt test and certification venues either. As long as you're willing to give it try, there are organizations and training clubs that are ready and willing to help.

Working Certificate Program

The Working Certificate (WC) program was developed by the Labrador Retriever Club (LRC) in 1931. The original intent of the LRC's WC program was to parallel that of the Kennel Club's program (in the United Kingdom). There, for a Labrador to be eligible for a conformation championship, the dog was required to pass a working test first.

The American Kennel Club, however, does not have the same requirement as the KC; a Lab doesn't need a WC—or any other hunting title—to be able to attain a championship. The LRC *does* require that before a *club member* puts the title of CH before his or her dog's name (even if the AKC has awarded the title), the Lab must earn a WC or an equivalent title (such as a Junior Hunter or placement at a field trial).

Working Certificate (WC)

The Working Certificate is a good test for novice owners who are interested in testing their dog's natural retrieving instincts. It doesn't involve a lot of training from the owner and, as with all retriever trials and tests, *the handler does not fire a shotgun. The shooting is left to official "gunners."*

To pass the Working Certificate test, the Lab must

1. not be gun-shy
2. successfully retrieve a shot bird 50 yards on land in light cover (usually tall grasses but nothing too difficult for the dog to run through);
3. successfully retrieve two ducks from water, one after the other; and
4. return the birds to within easy reach of the handler.

Owners who have never worked with retrieving dogs before and who are interested in working toward this

ACTIVITIES Hunt Test Organizations

American Kennel Club

Hunting Retriever Club/United Kennel Club*

North American Hunting Retriever Association

*The HRC/UKC hunt tests require that the handler fire a shotgun as if shooting the bird. A "popper" is used in the gun (as opposed to live ammunition), but proper gun handling is required. Participants are encouraged to attend an approved hunter safety course.

working certificate should find a training club in their area. A good point of contact would be a local Labrador Retriever club. The local club usually has a group that trains, or knows how to put you in contact with a training group for retrievers.

Working Certificate Excellent (WCX)

Many local and regional Labrador Retriever clubs offer a more advanced version of the LRC's working certificate, too. The Working Certificate Excellent (WCX) requires a little more from the dog. For example, such as the dog must retrieve *to hand* (directly to the owner's hand and not kinda sorta in the general area). The dog must also be able to retrieve the following:

1. Double (two) land-shot birds in light cover (75 yards); and
2. Double water-shot ducks from swimming water (the water is deep enough that the dog can't touch bottom and must swim).

As with the WC, only one "passing" score is required to earn the WCX certificate.

Hunt Tests

Hunt tests were developed to give owners a chance to test their dogs' retrieving abilities in noncompetitive tests that most closely simulate realistic hunting conditions. For those owners who want the adrenaline rush of competing (on a pass/fail basis), the pride of earning coveted titles, and the camaraderie of other Lab owners and handlers who are seeking the same things, hunt tests are the perfect venue for the novice.

Retriever hunt tests are run by the AKC, the Hunting Retriever Club (a division of the United Kennel Club [UKC]), and the North American Hunting Retriever Association (NAHRA).

All organizations offer testing at an entry or beginner level, as well as at intermediate and advanced levels.

The tests have different requirements and the scoring for pass/fail differs; however, the tests are similar enough that some Lab owners compete in more than one organization's program. The beginner and starter levels of the NAHRA hunt test program are described below.

Beginner

This is a perfect place for a novice handler to begin. These tests are informal and are set up as a straightforward, short single retrieve. The dog can be restrained on a leash at the line (starting point) and the Lab needs to retrieve the bird "within a reasonable radius" of the handler. The emphasis is on having *fun* and encouraging owners to continue to train and advance in the hunting tests. If your Labby passes, you receive an NAHRA Certificate of Merit.

Started

Delivery to hand is not required and a leash, line, or slip cord can be used to keep the dog steady at the line. This test involves five single marks:

- Two single marks on land (75 yards or less)
- Two single marks on water (50 yards or less)
- A fifth mark, either land or water (per judge's choice)

To achieve a Started Retriever (SR) title, the Lab must qualify (pass with a score of 80 percent or greater) in four tests.

More advanced tests are also available to the retriever: A Working Retriever (WR) certificate is awarded to the dog that has earned four qualifying scores at the *Intermediate* testing level; a Master Hunting Retriever (MHR) certificate for five qualifying scores in the *Senior* testing category, or a WR title and four qualifying *Senior* tests; and a Grand Master Hunting Retriever (GMHR) certificate awarded to a dog receiving 15 qualifying *Senior* tests.

Field Trials

The Labrador Retriever Club held the first field trial for retrievers on December 21, 1931. The field trial was run on an 18,000-acre estate in Chester, New York. It was held purposely on a Monday so that the event, which included many of the East Coast's wealthy estate owners, would not attract a "gallery" or audience.

Field trials have come a long way from being a sport of the elite. Today, more than 200 licensed field trials are held each year in the United States, and the events draw the most highly trained, competitive Labrador trainers and their dogs in the country.

Field trials *are not* for the faint of heart, those with easily bruised feelings, or the truly inexperienced, novice handler with a very "green" dog. Nonprofessional trainers and handlers can enter dogs in an "Amateur" stake (class), but keep in mind there can be a fine line between what most people consider an amateur (someone who competes for fun, as a hobby, and doesn't benefit monetarily) and who is allowed to compete as an amateur.

Field trials have been criticized as presenting hunting situations that are so far from reality that they don't represent what the Labrador Retriever was originally bred for anymore.

There's truth in this, but there's also a reason for it.

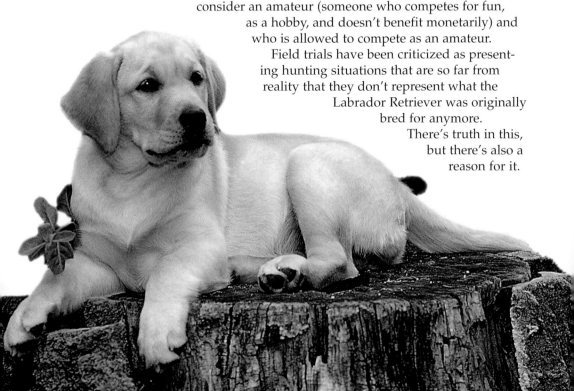

Field trials today are not what they were in the 1930s. The reason why the stakes within field trials have become increasingly difficult is that too many Labradors were capable of performing the stakes flawlessly. Field trials must place the dogs, first through fourth. In order to determine winners in each stake, the tests had to become more complex, the marks became longer, and the number of retrieves increased.

Labrador trainers and their dogs continued to rise to the challenge and continued to produce dogs that could complete the required retrieves perfectly. So, field trials upped the ante and continued to make the retrieves even more difficult.

Are field trials at a point where they no longer represent normal hunting situations? Yes, but as you can see, this transformation occurred over time and was in response to extremely skilled trainers and an incredible retriever.

Fun Facts

A professional trainer will often come to a retriever field trial with up to 20 dogs to handle for other owners.

If you're competitive, have a tough skin, and really enjoy the demands of this level of competition, and your Lab is field-trial material (the successful field-trial dog has been bred specifically for this event), you will want to contact your local Lab club for advice on where to train and with whom to train.

Be forewarned that training is so specialized for field trials that most first-time handlers (and many seasoned handlers) will opt to send their dogs to a professional trainer to have him "started." The novice will then train with the pro and his dog to learn how to handle the dog in field trials.

Get Wet!

If you've got a Lab that *loves* to retrieve, and loves to retrieve even more if water is involved, then you've got to check out perhaps the most fun competition known to retrievers: jumping off a dock into a pool of water to retrieve a favorite fetch toy.

In the DockDogs Big Air competition, the Lab that jumps the farthest distance off the dock to retrieve his fetch toy wins. In the Extreme Vertical competition, the dog that jumps the highest off the dock to grab the bumper (and drop into the water below) wins. And, there's also a division for the fastest retrieve in water, called what else? Speed Retrieve.

Fun Facts

The first DockDogs event was televised on ESPN's *Great Outdoor Games* in 2000.

According to DockDogs, distances are accurately measured with "a proprietary advanced digital video capture with digitally enhanced measurement systems software developed for use in Olympic events." The system scores each jump at the point where the dog's tail-set or hind end enters the water.

The measurement system may be high-tech, but the coolest thing about the DockDogs competition is that it is made for dogs and their owners. The goal of DockDogs is to get family pets out of the backyard and having fun. No prior experience is needed. You don't need a $10,000 professionally trained retriever to compete at the national or world levels. In fact, anyone with a dog and a fetch toy can participate. All breeds and mixes are allowed to participate; however, Labradors rule in this sport! The growth of this sport has mushroomed. In 2008, more than 100 DockDogs events were held.

Resources

Kennel and Breed Clubs

American Kennel Club (AKC)
5580 Centerview Drive
Raleigh, NC 27606-3390
(919) 233-9767
www.akc.org; *info@akc.org*

Canadian Kennel Club
200 Ronson Drive, Suite 400
Etobicoke, Ontario CANADA
M9W 5Z9
(416) 675-5511
www.ckc.ca

The Kennel Club (United Kingdom)
1-5 Clarges Street
Piccadilly, London W1J 8AB
0870 606 6750
www.thekennelclub.org.uk

Fédération Cynologique Internationale
FCI Office
Place Albert 1er, 13
B-6530 THUIN
BELGIQUE
Tél : ++32.71.59.12.38
www.fci.be

United Kennel Club (UKC)
100 East Kilgore Road
Kalamazoo, MI 49002-5584
(269) 343-9020
www.ukcdogs.com

Labrador Retriever Club, Inc. (AKC)
www.thelabradorclub.com
inquiry@thelabradorclub.com

Labrador Retriever Club (KC/UK)
www.thelabradorretrieverclub.com

Labrador Retriever Club of Canada (CKC)
c/o Mary-Anne Lauzon, Membership
800 Eadie Road
Russell, Ontario K4R 1E5
www.labrador-canada.com

National Labrador Retriever Club (FCI)
Deb Arnold, Membership Chair
twin_cedars@prodigy.net
www.nationallabradorretrieverclub.com

United Labrador Retriever
    Association (ULRA)
P.O. Box 1704
Conover, NC 28613
www.ulra.net
info@ulra.net

Yellow Labrador Retriever Club
    (United Kingdom)
www.yellowlabclub.co.uk
sussiewiles@yahoo.co.uk

Health Organizations

Canine Eye Registration
    Foundation (CERF)
Veterinary Medical DataBases-
    VMDB/CERF
1717 Philo Road
P.O. Box 3007
Urbana, IL 61803-3007
(217) 693-4800
www.vmdb.org/cerf.html

Canine Health Information
    Center (CHIC)
2300 E. Nifong Blvd.
Columbia, MO 65201-3806
(573) 442-0418
www.caninehealthinfo.org/chicinfo.htm

Orthopedic Foundation for
    Animals (OFA)
2300 E. Nifong Blvd.
Columbia, MO 65201-3806
(573) 442-0418
www.offa.org
ofa@offa.org

University of Pennsylvania Hip
    Improvement Program
    (PennHip)
Veterinary Hospital of University of
    Pennsylvania
3900 Delancey Street
Philadelphia, PA 19104-6010
(215) 898-4680
www.pennhip.org

Activities/Behavior

Agility
American Kennel Club (AKC)
See listing under "Organizations."

Canine Performance Events, Inc.
    (CPE)
P.O. Box 805
South Lyon, MI 48178
www.k9cpe.com; cpe@charter.net

North American Dog Agility
    Council (NADAC)
P.O. Box 1206
Colbert, OK 74733
www.nadac.com; info@nadac.com

United Kennel Club (UKC)
See listing under "Organizations."

United States Dog Agility
    Association (USDAA)
P.O. Box 850995
Richardson, TX 75085
(972) 487-2200
www.usdaa.com; info@usdaa.com

Animal-assisted Therapy
The Delta Society
875 124th Ave. NE, Suite 101
Bellevue, WA 98005-2531
(425) 679-5500
www.deltasociety.org
info@deltasociety.org

Therapy Dogs International, Inc.
88 Bartley Road
Flanders, NJ 07836
(973) 252-9800
www.tdi-dog.org; tdi@gti.net

**R.E.A.D. (Reading Education
Assistance Program)**
Intermountain Therapy Animals
P.O. Box 17201
Salt Lake City, UT 84117
(801) 272-3439
*www.therapyanimals.org/read;
info@therapyanimals.org*

Behavior/Training
Animal Behavior Society
Indiana University
2611 East 10th Street
Bloomington, IN 47408-2603
(812) 856-5541
*www.animalbehavior.org;
aboffice@indiana.edu*

**American College of Veterinary
Behaviorists (ACVB)**
A listing of all current Diplomates
from the ACVB are listed on the
organization's web site at
www.dacvb.org.

**American Veterinary Medical
Association**
1931 North Meacham Road,
Suite 100
Schaumburg, IL 60173-4360
(847) 925-8070
www.avma.org; avmainfo@avma.org

**Association of Pet Dog Trainers
(APDT)**
150 Executive Center Drive, Box 35
Greenville, SC 29615
(800) PET-DOGS
www.apdt.com; information@apdt.com

**International Association of
Canine Professionals**
P.O. Box 560156
Montverde, FL 34756-0156
(877) THE-IACP
*www.dogpro.org
iacpadmin@mindspring.com*

**National Association of Dog
Obedience Instructors**
PMB 369
729 Grapevine Hwy.
Hurst, TX 76054-2085
www.nadoi.org; corrsec2@nadoi.org

Canine Good Citizen
See "American Kennel Club" listing.

Conformation
See "American Kennel Club" listing.
See "United Kennel Club" listing.

DockDogs
5183 Silver Maple Lane
Medina, OH 44256
(330) 241-4975
*www.dockdogs.com
info@dockdogs.com*

Field Trials/Hunt Tests
See "American Kennel Club" listing.

**Hunting Retriever Club/
United Kennel Club**
*www.huntingretriever.org
AdminSecretary@H-R-C.org*
Also see "United Kennel Club"
listing.

North American Hunting Retriever Association
P.O. Box 5159
Fredericksburg, VA 22403
(540) 899-7620
www.nahranews.net

Flyball
North American Flyball Association
1400 West Devon Avenue, #512
Chicago, IL 60660
(800) 318-6312
www.flyball.org; flyball@flyball.org

Musical Freestyle
World Canine Freestyle Organization
P.O. Box 350122
Brooklyn, NY 11235
(718) 332-8336
www.worldcaninefreestyle.org
wdfodogs@aol.com

Musical Dog Sport Association
9211 West Road, #143-104
Houston, TX 77064
www.musicaldogsport.com

Obedience
See "American Kennel Club" listing.
See "United Kennel Club" listing.

Rally
See "American Kennel Club" listing.
See "Association of Pet Dog Trainers."

Search and Rescue
National Association for Search and Rescue, Inc.
Education Services Director,
    Janet Adere
(703) 222-6277
www.nasar.org
janeta@nasar.org

Tracking
See "American Kennel Club" listing.

Galleries
William Secord Gallery, Inc.
52 East 76th Street
New York, NY 10021
(877) 249-DOGS
www.dogpainting.com

Museum of the Dog
1721 S. Mason Road
St. Louis, MO 63131
(314) 821-3647
www.museumofthedog.org

The National Sporting Library
102 The Plains Road
Middleburg, VA 20118-1335
(540) 687-6542
www.nsl.org.

Books

Art
Secord, William. *Dog Painting, 1840–1940, A Social History of the Dog in Art.* Suffolk, England: Antique Collector's Club, 2003.
————. *A Breed Apart: The Art Collections of the American Kennel Club and The American Kennel Club Museum of The Dog.* Suffolk, England: Antique Collector's Club, 2001.

Blind Dogs
Levin, RN, and Caroline D. *Living with Blind Dogs.* Oregon City, OR: Lantern Publications, 2003.

Massage

Fox, Michael W. *The Healing Touch for Dogs*. New York: Newmarket Press, 2004.

Tellington-Jones, Linda. *Getting in Touch with Your Dog*. Roxbury, ME: Kenilworth Press, 2006.

Activities

Agility

Canova, Ali, Diane Goodspeed, Joe Canova, and Bruce Curtis. *Agility Training for You and Your Dog: From Backyard Fun to High-Performance Training*. Guilford, CT: Globe Pequot Press, 2008.

Simmons-Moake, Jane. *Agility Training, the Fun Sport for All Dogs*. New York: Howell Book House, 1992.

Simmons-Moake, Jane. *Excelling at Dog Agility: Book 1: Obstacle Training*. Houston: Flashpaws Productions, 1999.

Animal-assisted Therapy

Burch, Mary R. *Wanted! Animal Volunteers*. New York: John Wiley & Sons, 2002.

Burch, Mary R., and Aaron Honori Katcher. *Volunteering with Your Pet: How to Get Involved in Animal-Assisted Therapy with Any Kind of Pet*. New York: John Wiley & Sons, 1996.

Howie, Ann R., Mary Burch, and Ellen Shay. *The Pet Partners Team Training Course: Pets Helping People Manual*. Seattle: Delta Society, 2001.

Canine Good Citizen

Volhard, Jack, and Wendy Volhard. *The Canine Good Citizen: Every Dog Can Be One*, 2nd Edition. New York: John Wiley & Sons, 1997.

Conformation

Coile, D. Caroline. *Show Me! A Dog Showing Primer*, 2nd Edition. Hauppauge, NY: Barron's Educational Series, Inc., 2009.

Ronchette, Vicki. *Positive Training for Show Dogs—Building a Relationship for Success*. Wenatchee, WA: Dogwise Publishing, 2007.

Smith, Cheryl S. *The Complete Guide to Showing Your Dog*. New York: Crown Publishing Group, 2001.

Flyball

Olson, Lonnie. *Flyball Racing: The Dog Sport for Everyone*. New York: John Wiley & Sons, 1997.

Parkin, Jacqueline. *Flyball Training—Start to Finish*. Crawford, CO: Alpine Publications, 1998.

Obedience

Anderson, Bobbie. *Building Blocks for Performance*. Crawford, CO: Alpine Publications, 2002.

Bauman, Diane L. *Beyond Basic Dog Training*. New York: John Wiley & Sons, 2003.

Spector, Morgan. *Clicker Training for Obedience: Shaping Top Performance Positively*. Waltham, MA: Sunshine Books, 1999.

Rally

Dearth, Janice. *The Rally Course Book: A Guide to AKC Rally Courses*. Crawford, CO: Alpine Publications, 2004.

Dennison, Pamela S. *Click Your Way to Rally Obedience*. Crawford, CO: Alpine Publications, 2006.

Kramer, Charles "Bud." *Rally-O: The Style of Rally Obedience*, 3rd Edition. Manhattan, KS: Fancee Publications, 2005.

Sawford, Marie. *Rally On*. Guelph, ON, Canada: Dog Sport Media, 2006.

Search and Rescue
American Rescue Dog Association. *Search and Rescue Dogs: Training the K-9 Hero*, 2nd Edition. New York: John Wiley & Sons, 2002.

Hammond, Shirley. *Training the Disaster Search Dog*. Wenatchee, WA: Dogwise Publishing, 2005.

Judah, J. C. *Building a Basic Foundation for Search and Rescue Dog Training*. Morrisville, NC: Lulu Publishing, 2007.

Tracking
Krause, Carolyn. *Try Tracking! The Puppy Tracking Primer*. Wenatchee, WA: Dogwise Publishing, 2005.

Sanders, William "Sil." *Enthusiastic Tracking: A Step by Step Training Handbook*. Stanwood, WA: Rime Publications, 1998.

Behavior/Training
General Dog Behavior
Aloff, Brenda. *Canine Body Language, A Photographic Guide*. Wenatchee, WA: Dogwise Publishing, 2005.

Bailey, PhD, Jon S., and Mary R. Burch. *How Dogs Learn*. New York: John Wiley & Sons, 1999.

Coren, Stanley. *How Dogs Think: What the World Looks Like to Them and Why They Act the Way They Do*. New York: Simon & Schuster, 2005.

———. *How to Speak Dog: Mastering the Art of Dog-Human Communication*, New York: Simon & Schuster, 2001.

Donaldson, Jean. *Oh Behave! Dogs from Pavlov to Premack to Pinker*. Wenatchee, WA: Dogwise Publishing, 2008.

Fogle, Bruce. *The Dog's Mind: Understanding Your Dog's Behavior*. New York: John Wiley & Sons, 1990.

McConnell, PhD, Patricia B. *The Other End of the Leash: Why We Do What We Do Around Dogs*. New York: Random House, 2003.

———. *For the Love of a Dog: Understanding Emotion in You and Your Best Friend*. New York: Random House, 2006.

Behavior (Problem)
Donaldson, Jean. *Mine! A Guide to Resource Guarding in Dogs*. San Francisco: Kinship Communications/SF-SPCA, 2002.

Killion, Jane. *When Pigs Fly: Training Success with Impossible Dogs*. Wenatchee, WA: Dogwise Publishing, 2007.

McConnell, PhD, Patricia B. *I'll Be Home Soon! How to Prevent and Treat Separation Anxiety*. Black Earth, WI: Dog's Best Friend, 2000.

———. *The Cautious Canine: How to Help Dogs Conquer Their Fears*. Black Earth, WI: Dog's Best Friend, 1998.

McConnell, PhD, Patricia B., and Karen B. London, PhD. *The Feisty Fido: Help for the Leash-Aggressive Dog*. Black Earth, WI: Dog's Best Friend, 2003.

Pryor, Karen. *Don't Shoot the Dog! The New Art of Teaching and Training*. Waltham, MA: Sunshine Books, 2006.

Rugass, Turid. *Barking: The Sound of a Language*. Wenatchee, WA: Dogwise Publishing, 2008.

———. *My Dog Pulls. What Do I Do?* Wenatchee, WA: Dogwise Publishing, 2005.

Training

Clicker Training

Book, Mandy, and Cheryl Smith. *Quick Clicks: 40 Fast and Fun Behaviors to Train with a Clicker*. Wenatchee, WA: Dogwise Publishing, 2001.

Pryor, Karen. *Click! Dog Training System*. (Book and clicker.) New York: Metro Books, 2007.

———. *Clicker Training for Dogs*, 4th Edition. Waltham, MA: Sunshine Books, 2005.

House Training

Kalstone, Shirlee. *How to Housebreak Your Dog in 7 Days*, 2nd Edition. New York: Bantam Books, 2004.

Palika, Liz. *The Pocket Idiot's Guide to Housetraining Your Dog*. New York: Penquin Group (USA), 2007.

Socializing with Dogs

Bennett, Robin, and Susan Briggs. *Off-leash Dog Play: A Complete Guide to Safety and Fun*. Woodbridge, VA: C&R Publishing, 2008.

McConnell, PhD, Patricia B. *Feeling Outnumbered? How to Manage and Enjoy Your Multi-dog Household* (expanded and updated edition). Black Earth, WI: Dog's Best Friend, 2008.

Socializing with People

Long, Lorie. *A Dog Who's Always Welcome: Assistance and Therapy Dog Trainers Teach You How to Socialize and Train Your Companion Dog*. New York: John Wiley & Sons, Inc., 2008.

McConnell, PhD, Patricia B. *How to Be the Leader of the Pack and Have Your Dog Love You for It!* Black Earth, WI: Dog's Best Friend, 1996.

Trick Training

Haggerty, Captain, and Arthur J. Haggerty. *How to Teach Your Dog to Talk: 125 Easy-to-Learn Tricks Guaranteed to Entertain Both You and Your Pet*. New York: Simon & Schuster: 2000.

Sundance, Kyra. *101 Dog Tricks: Step-by-Step Activities to Engage, Challenge and Bond with Your Dog*. Bloomington, IN: Quarry Books, 2007.

Labrador Retriever Magazines

LRC Newsletter
(subscription through LRC Web site)

The Labrador Quarterly
Hoflin Publishing, Inc.
4401 Zephyr St.
Wheat Ridge, CO 80033
www.hoflin.com/Magazines/ TheLabradorQuarterly.html)

Retriever News
4379 S. Howell Ave., Suite 17
Milwaukee, WI 53207-5053
www.working-retriever.com/ rftnform.html

Index

THE TEAM BEHIND THE *TRAIN YOUR DOG* DVD

Host **Nicole Wilde** is a certified Pet Dog Trainer and internationally recognized author and lecturer. Her books include *So You Want to be a Dog Trainer* and *Help for Your Fearful Dog* (Phantom Publishing). In addition to working with dogs, Nicole has been working with wolves and wolf hybrids for over fifteen years and is considered an expert in the field.

Host **Laura Bourhenne** is a Professional Member of the Association of Pet Dog Trainers, and holds a degree in Exotic Animal Training. She has trained many species of animals including several species of primates, birds of prey, and many more. Laura is striving to enrich the lives of pets by training and educating the people they live with.

Director **Leo Zahn** is an award winning director/cinematographer/editor of television commercials, movies, and documentaries. He has directed and edited more than a dozen instructional DVDs through the Picture Company, a subsidiary of Picture Palace, Inc., based in Los Angeles.

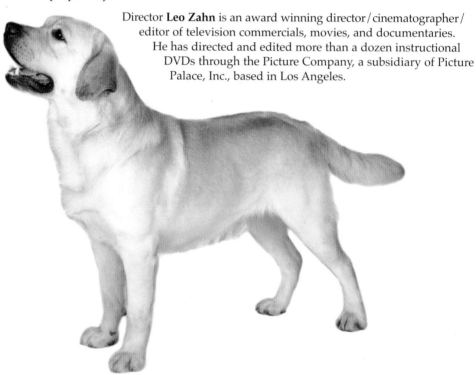